the chocolate effect

healing miracles of chocolate and compassion

by

Arun Sardana

ISBN:0692069933
ISBN-13:9780692069936

DEDICATED TO

My father, Krishan Chandra Sardana, for all the lessons that he taught me through his keen wisdom, deep intellect, intense suffering, and the most loving smile.

I love you dad and I miss you dearly. Your spirit will always live inside me.

CONTENTS

acknowledgments   i

about this book   3

1   the river's message   14

2   the awakening   32

3   birth of The Gap   48

4   ego and hubris   64

5   anxiety, fear and depression   79

6   sex and sin   94

7   love, marriage and divorce   117

8   anger's wrath   136

9   illness, suicide and death   151

10   sorrow, grief and despair   168

11   forgiveness, gratitude, humility and prayer   182

12   Gu-Ru – out of darkness, into the Light   195

ACKNOWLEDGMENTS

While the triggers of awakening may lie inside us, the sparks to ignite this fire are generally present around us. My sources of inspiration are similarly connected to me through bonds of love, respect and admiration.

First and foremost, I would like to express my sincere gratitude to Neha, Nikita and Ratna – the three most important women in my life – who have always offered unbound love and support during this journey. They have taught me important lessons about self-awareness and what it means to be human. The joy they have given me through their unconditional affection is beyond the grasp of vocabulary and glowing words. I am deeply grateful to the Creator that my life was blessed by their presence.

My sincere thanks also go to my spiritual guides and angel spirits who brought surprise insights that helped me gradually shift the lens through which I view this world. They include my friends, colleagues, teachers, and coaches – far too many to name here – who were always there to answer the last of my lingering questions.

Last but not least, I offer my humble obeisance to Mother Nature that has unleashed a flood of inspirations and has provided clarity to complex questions that had plagued me for a very long time. It gives me comfort to know that I will eventually return to Her when all my remaining questions will be answered forever.

about this book

This book is not a work of scientific theories or of scientific convictions. This is a spiritual book, first and foremost. It is an attempt to better understand the construct of human conditions such as anger, anxiety, grief, sex, sin, and even suicide through a lens of compassion and spirituality. As such, the text touches on subjects that are still mysterious and awe-inspiring, even though science is making attempts to better understand them. This book is neither an endeavor to find a universal answer to suffering nor an indifference to existing ways of coping with pain. It is also not an effort to challenge science, religious beliefs, or personal ideologies. Rather, it is an expression of my personal sensibilities and lessons I have learned through trials and tribulations. I struggled for a long time to decide if this work should be published or even written because it necessitated that I become vulnerable and that I share parts of my life that only a handful of people know about. In fact, some portions of my life and the internal dialogue that I disclose here will be news to my family and close friends. They were my dark secrets ... until now.

I have used expressions such as Creator, God, Inner Self, Higher Self, Supreme Power, and Higher Consciousness as declarations of the mysterious power that is much bigger, more creative, and more powerful than any one of us and all of us combined. The use of female gender in representing a person was simply out of respect for the spirituality that a woman represents. After all, only a female can nurture and bring new life into this world.

This book was written with a singular goal: to offer an alternative way of thinking about suffering associated with different human conditions—from anger, anxiety, fear, and depression, to love, marriage, divorce, and suicide—so that we can use a different lens than what society has traditionally provided. Clearly, there are many more human states that cause pain and suffering—hate, envy, jealousy, regret, animosity, and resentment, to name a few—that are not addressed here. Perhaps they will be covered in another book. However, the lens that I have presented could be used to view any and all such conditions to better understand them, with compassion.

I am convinced that the path to end suffering can be accessed through simple and pragmatic acts of compassion such as those offered in this work. Before you reach the same conclusion, or a different one, I feel it is my responsibility to share with you the small kernel of truth that I have found and that I share with you through this writing. After reading this book, some may agree and identify with what I experienced, and others may consider this account completely worthless. Both viewpoints are valid since they are derived through our very personal lens of beliefs, values, and convictions. Please join me on this humbling journey with an open mind so that our voyage together can be mutually enriching. All I request from you is simply your curiosity.

My sincere hope is that you will find my observations and awareness useful in your personal quest to understand human suffering, to heal and to attain the peace and happiness that eludes most, if not all, of us.

Finally, this book is not an effort to enrich my personal coffers. All profits from the sale of this book will be used to provide assistance to abandoned and abused children so that they can have a fair chance at life. I hope you will join me in this healing journey.

what is the chocolate effect?

the chocolate effect is a metaphor for transforming suffering into happiness through compassion. As the title of the book suggests, there's an unmistakable overlap between what Mayans knew many centuries ago about Xocolatl (show-co-la-til), the cocoa drink that they called the "food of the gods" and what Buddha knew over 2600 years ago about compassion. If you lived during the time of Montezuma, the 16th century Aztec emperor, who consumed inordinate amounts of the cocoa drink before entering his harem, you would probably believe that cocoa had only one physical benefit for men. Women, on the other hand, were prohibited from consuming this drink during the Mayan and Aztec era because of its purported aphrodisiacal qualities. It seems that men, since time immemorial, have been insecure about giving women equal rights even for the natural physical pleasures.

It wasn't until 1828 when the Dutch chemist Coenraad Johannes van Houten invented the cocoa press that the price of chocolate started to drop and it became available to men and women alike. Compassion on the other hand has been part of our genetic make-up and natural behavior from the beginning of time. Its expression does not require the ingestion of any manmade compound. The Creator made it readily available to us in unlimited quantities, naturally and without any gender discrimination.

What Olmecs, Mayans and Aztecs knew experientially about the invigorating, mood enhancing benefit of their treasured spicy cocoa drink, modern science had to find convincing evidence for it. One doesn't need science to know that having a piece of silky smooth chocolate simply feels good. Science, however, has gone further and found the miracle compound called flavanol in cocoa used to make dark chocolate (sorry milk chocolate lovers – you are out of luck because flavanol has been mostly processed out of your delectable delight). As reported by Cleveland Clinic, "Flavanols are the main type of flavonoid found in cocoa and chocolate. In addition to having antioxidant qualities, research shows that flavanols have other potential influences on vascular health, such as lowering blood pressure, improving blood flow to the brain and heart..." If you thought that lowering blood pressure and improving blood flow to the brain must result in some cognitive benefits also, then you would be absolutely right.

In one of the most intriguing studies I came across while doing research on chocolate, Franz H. Messerli, M.D., argued that chocolate improves cognitive function by showing a high correlation between number of Nobel Prize winners of a country and the country's total chocolate consumption. If you are aspiring to win a Nobel Prize, you may want to consult your doctor before you start consuming inordinate amounts of chocolate like Montezuma, arguably for a nobler purpose.

Harvard Health Letter, a publication of Harvard Medical

School, also reported the results of a few studies conducted with cocoa flavanols. These studies showed improved cognitive function even among those who had mild cognitive impairment. As Dr. Miguel Alonso-Alonso, a neuroscientist at Beth Israel Deaconess Medical Center says, "From laboratory and animal studies, we know that flavanols facilitate brain cell connections and survival, and protect brain cells from toxins or the negative effects of inflammation."

Studies by respected scientists and journalists from various credible organizations, citing no conflict of interest, have shown other benefits of consuming flavanols including heart health, mood improvement, reducing symptoms of depression, risk reduction of strokes in women, and in helping seniors reduce memory loss. Some critics are not convinced. So, the COSMOS or The Cocoa Supplement and Multivitamin Outcomes Study at Brigham and Women's Hospital was started in 2017 with 18,000 participants in an effort to confirm (or refute) what Mesoamericans have known for centuries. As reported by the MARS Center for Cocoa Health Sciences, "The study will investigate whether taking daily supplements of cocoa flavanols (600mg/day) or a common multivitamin reduces the risk for developing heart disease, stroke, and cancer."

While we await the results of this clinical trial, we don't

have to wait for compassion's documented benefits that are strikingly comparable to those of cocoa and chocolate. Similar to the mood enhancing benefits of chocolate, the evidence shows that compassion and genuine happiness go hand-in-hand. Unlike cocoa and chocolate though, you can tap into your compassion reserves for free. Better still, compassion multiplies with practice and its expression reaps large bounties of sociological, psychological and physiological benefits.

Our craving to tap into compassion may be just as strong as our yearning for chocolate. As reported in the archives of the Association for Psychological Sciences, researchers at the Max Planck Institute in Germany found that human infants and chimpanzees will not only engage in helpful behavior but will overcome obstacles to do so. Even more importantly, they display this behavior without the expectation of any reward or selfless compassion.

Perhaps, one of the most powerful evidence of how compassion affects our physiology and psychology, in ways similar to chocolate, is the fascinating study conducted by Steve Cole of University of California, Los Angeles, and Barbara Frederickson of University of North Carolina, Chapel Hill. Cole and Frederickson measured cellular inflammation as a proxy for happiness among people who described themselves as "very happy." Cellular inflammation has a high correlation to psychological stress and killer disease like cancer among others. They expected inflammation at the cellular level to be lower among "very happy" people because of lower stress levels. What they discovered was scientifically significant – inflammation was lower but only among a certain group of happy people. Those who found happiness in hedonic, material pleasures displayed high inflammation compared to those who were happy because they lived a life of meaning and purpose. The lives of the latter group were focused on helping others rather than simply satisfying their wants and needs. Their lives were defined by altruism, empathy and selfless compassion, just like the human infants and chimpanzees.

The story gets better. Low inflammation means lower stress and perhaps lower incidence of disease. These, in turn, could affect our longevity. In other words, a desire to positively impact the lives of others has the power to enhance our own lifespan. Research conducted by Dr. Sara Konrath of University of Michigan discovered the truth behind this statement – that those who engaged in volunteerism lived longer than those who did not but with an important caveat. This was true only if the volunteers had no ulterior motive but simply a desire to positively impact the life of others. So, a simple act of writing a check to a charity for tax deduction purposes is unlikely to increase your lifespan. You can certainly buy more chocolate with the tax refund but giving it away selflessly might bring more durable happiness than consuming it yourself. Don't believe me, there's scientific evidence for it.

With advances in technology, researchers can now better understand why compassion has this affect on our psyche and our physiology. Jordan Grafman of National Institutes of Health found that brain scans of people receiving money or observing others giving money to charity showed a similar amount of activity in their brain's "pleasure center." Pleasure center is the part of the brain that lights up when we experience pleasures brought on by eating our favorite food, engaging in sexual activity, or feeling happy on receiving a large tax refund. Giving, in other words, was just as pleasurable as receiving, if not more so. We have all experienced how giving feeds our soul with a deep sense of joy and peace. Moral of the story is simple – share your chocolate and your pleasure center will light up even more. That's compassion at work.

This study has other important implications that go beyond just the obvious conclusion, in my opinion. Once we start experiencing eudemonic happiness that selfless service brings, then it is only a matter of time that we become an addict of compassion. As we will see, this addiction perhaps holds the best chance of placing us on the path of durable happiness and inner peace.

If you still have doubts about the power of compassion but you believe in the power of true love, then this single fact alone may change your mind. A study completed recently showed that one of the most highly desirable traits that men and women seek alike in a romantic relationship is kindness, compassion's close first cousin. Certainly chocolate helps too.

Producing something as delectable a treat as chocolate requires several harsh steps that include splitting the cocoa pods with machetes, fermenting the cocoa beans, drying them for days in the hot sun followed by roasting at high temperatures, grinding the nibs into a paste and then conching it before the final product is ready to be tempered and molded. The harsh journey of a coffee bean is an apt metaphor for the suffering a human being endures during a lifetime. If only cocoa beans could express their feelings while they are being roasted and ground, their story wouldn't be very different from our own narrative. What makes cocoa beans' difficult passage bearable is the loving care they receive at every step of the process. If it wasn't for this extraordinary attention and love, we may never taste the natural essence of the cocoa nibs in a smooth, delectable bar of chocolate. Similarly, compassion for the self and for others can help us mortals through many of life's trying journeys so that our natural essence and character can be revealed.

Hopefully, you are convinced enough that chocolate and compassion can offer healing miracles that can transform our lives, and that of others. Now let's examine how the lens of compassion can transform our view of personal suffering. As we do that, let's also enjoy some dark chocolate. It may just bring a miracle or two in our lives.

1

the river's message

Life's storms have an intensity and fury that can only be matched by love and divinity. And their aftereffects are filled with serenity.

Five days before my twenty-third birthday, my father suffered a debilitating stroke that trapped his incredibly intelligent mind in a body that stopped obeying its orders. Five months later, he committed suicide. Three months before my thirty-ninth birthday, memories of childhood sexual abuse came flooding in out of nowhere. Life, as I knew it, was no longer the same. The happiness and peace that I regularly experienced as a child and young adult was sapped by the troubling memories of these traumatic events. It all seemed like a bad dream that I could not wake from. I felt emotionally suffocated and exhausted. I contemplated ending my life, but the love of my family kept me from repeating my father's desperate action.

I was born into a Hindu family, but like my mother, practiced Sikhism from a very early age. While religion and spirituality came to me naturally, I was always introspective and yearned for more knowledge. This spiritual thirst did not go unnoticed by my mother. She explained this curiosity by the fact that I shared my date of birth with one of the Sikh gurus, Guru Gobind Singh. She would proudly mention this fact to the priest every year when the Guru's birthday was celebrated. She was convinced that somehow I was deeply connected to Him. A mother's love and admiration for her children is truly unbound.

Growing up in India in a traditional, conservative, patriarchal family was full of comfort and laughter on the surface with deep-seated anxiety and fear primarily because of my father's unpredictable mood swings and bouts of uncontrollable anger. The temperature in our home was measured by the expressions on his face when he woke up in the morning and when he arrived home from a long day of work in the evening. This anxiety was compounded by deep financial uncertainty, as my father's efforts to establish a dependable business never took root, and we were in a constant state of flux, as he switched at least six business lines before his death. While I can now understand his extreme frustration and anger as a "failed" father, the memories of domestic violence and abuse have carved their permanent imprint on my psyche.

I was an above-average student and, to my father's credit, he somehow found ways to keep his three children in expensive private schools. A good education was not negotiable, and I lived up to my father's expectations. I looked forward to showing my grade report to him since it always meant that we were going to have a few relaxed and happy moments at home. It troubles me when I think that my father, like everyone else, wanted to be happy, and desperately so, but life's circumstance wouldn't let him get there for any sustained period of time. Gradually, the daily stresses of life that were outside his control translated into physical and mental disease, which ultimately pushed him to do what he could control—end his misery and suffering with death.

Six months after my father's passing, the family's financial distress and a deep- rooted desire to migrate to the land of opportunity—the United States of America—triggered my departure from India. Armed with a three-month leave from my promising and fun job managing a restaurant and an exclusive members-only discotheque at a luxury 5-star hotel, all my savings totaling a whopping $200, and fears and dreams as big as the Titanic, I arrived in the US. This was supposed to be a fact-finding trip to potentially establish a home base in the US, but the Universe had something else in mind. I found a job, was awarded a work permit, and thus began my journey to achieve the American Dream. I married a beautiful woman who became my pride and joy. I loved her dearly, even though we had an arranged marriage. Her parents had trusted me enough to send her from

India to the United States, and she was now my responsibility. I purchased our starter home before she arrived so we could begin our life together. We both worked hard and saved for a secure future. We imagined a beautiful, successful life with the laughter of children filling our home. Over the next few years, we were blessed with two beautiful angels—our daughters, Neha and Nikita. My mission to succeed materially assumed a different dimension after my first daughter was born. Emotional scars caused by my father's suicide had to wait to heal. I had not yet become aware of my childhood sexual abuse— that ugly memory awakened from the deep recesses of my brain during a wedding celebration in the glorious mountains of Vermont in 2004. In fact, as my therapist explained many years later, I had zipped up all my traumas subconsciously and put them away somewhere deep inside. Now they were becoming unzipped. Before this time, the stakes of financial peril and pure survival in an adopted country were way too high, and failure was not an option.

I was intoxicated by material wealth. It made me feel relevant, in control, powerful. It was how I thought I could express my love for my family—by giving them the security and comfort that I lacked in my youth—something my father was unable to provide despite his best and, at times, herculean efforts. Providing material comforts for my loved ones became a definition of love for me. I thought that it made me a good father, a good husband, a good sibling, a good friend, a loving caretaker. In fact, as I realized later, it was the perfect veil to hide my personal narrative of suffering, internal turmoil, and emptiness. I stayed busy making money so I did not have to make peace with my soul. Homes, luxury cars, jewelry, custom-made clothes and expensive vacations—I wanted it all and earned it. I achieved the American Dream and even more with the integrity that my father had imbibed in me. Like countless others who arrive in this great country with nothing but fears, hopes, and dreams and achieve much, my life was also labeled a quintessential immigrant success story.

However, not unlike many who achieve material success, I could feel a gaping hole deep inside me. I would lie awake late at night, and my wife would sometimes ask what was wrong. I would answer, "God has blessed us with more than we could ever imagine possible. We have two beautiful daughters, a nice home, all material comforts, and a job I absolutely love. But I feel empty inside. Like there's a hollow space in my soul that I cannot fill. Something is missing, but I don't know what?" Since my wife knew my father when he was alive, she would simply say, "You think too much ... just like your father. Stop thinking and go to sleep." To be fair, this conversation generally occurred at 2:00 a.m., and all she wanted was some peaceful sleep. She meant well, but I got more perturbed when she mentioned my father, as scenes from that fateful day of his death would come flooding in. Emotional dams would crack and, more often than not, completely break down releasing torments of anger, self-pity, guilt, and unbearable sadness.

Once the emotional waters would subside, I would be plagued by the same questions that torment many others. I would ask these questions of myself in my own head or of God in the only other safe place—the gurudwara, the place of worship for Sikhs. Why is there pain in our heart that leaves us unfulfilled regardless of all the material blessings? Why do we suffer? Why can't the physical and sensual pleasures of this world heal our pain? Why is "success" so hollow? If we are aware that money cannot buy happiness, why do we continue to crave more and more of it? Why are we so restless all the time? Why are we filled with anxiety and fear despite having all the material comforts and our loving families and friends around us? Why can't we find lasting peace and happiness? What bothered me the most was my belief system in the concept of sin as many roads led me to the same conclusion—that peace would always elude me due to my past sinful actions.

I had been a good son, father, husband, brother, and friend—a good person without malice or hatred toward anyone. But, I believed that I had sinned and that my father's suicide was God's punishment for my despicable acts. How could I have been punished so severely for my past karmā or deeds from previous lives. Where was the evidence for such reasoning? I questioned silently. I wondered if this was indeed the message of our Gurus, or was it simply the interpretation of their preaching by insecure religious leaders who sought control and compliance of unsuspecting followers? After all, how could anyone get into the head of the Buddha or Guru Nanak and truly know what they were thinking when they preached their sermons?

So, I decided to read incessantly about every religion to try to better understand the construct of suffering. What puzzled me most was the paradox created by the basic assumption of most religions that God lives inside us. If we are the embodiment of our Creator, our God, who is sublime, pure, and beyond reproach, then who commits the sin? And who experiences this suffering? If our physical body experiences vision, hearing, taste, smell, and touch, then it must also be the body that experiences suffering, I reasoned rather unintelligently. But not all suffering is physical in nature. Much of it, in fact, is emotional and embedded deep inside, perhaps where God lives. How could our physical existence cause so much emotional suffering to something so serene and sacred—our soul, our consciousness, our inner being? This disconnect bothered me.

As I continued my quest for answers, I discovered that Buddha and the enlightened souls who either preceded him or followed him had already solved much of this puzzle, but one critical aspect remained unanswered for me. In Buddha's translated works, the Pali Canon, the Buddhist literary monks agree that one source of suffering is our craving for the physical, limited world, which is transient and impermanent. The question I had always asked was *why?* *Why* do we crave and continue to chase the material and sensual pleasures in the name of happiness despite our awareness that they ultimately cause suffering? If fire burns us, we know it will hurt us if we touch it again, so we don't dare touch the flames. Why then, after repeated failures, do we keep repeating our actions that cause suffering to the eternal? This central question kept gnawing at me unforgivingly, even as strains were beginning to appear in my marriage of eighteen years because our spiritual growth was on very divergent paths. My wife had a more pragmatic view of life and spirituality in general—she prescribed to the theory of fate, acceptance and surrender—while I was questioning the very meaning of our existence in my quest to discover the reason I was placed on this earth.

The first clue to solving this puzzle came in the most unexpected way. During a particularly tumultuous visit to Costa Rica in April 2009 after the passing of my mother the previous year, I found myself standing near the banks of what seemed like an angry, muddy river, flowing furiously toward the ominous gray ocean after an early morning tropical thunderstorm. The blustery weather perfectly reflected the turbulent state of my mind. I never really got a chance to grieve the passing of my parents. I also had not confronted the issues around my sexual abuse. There were other priorities on which our family's survival depended. Maybe that was just a convenient excuse to not open any Pandora's box lest I discover something even darker. Watching the river's fury flooded me with a rush of emotions. I was thankful that it was still raining lightly, as it was a natural mask for tears. I stood motionless in the rain and thought that the river was the perfect metaphor for my life—furious, angry, rushing, and muddy.

Exhausted emotionally, I sat by the river's side pondering this strange similarity when the song of the river brought a different insight. The river told me that our lives couldn't be more dissimilar. While the self-created narrative of shame, guilt, and self-pity imprisoned me, she was a free spirit, singing joyfully and dancing in ecstasy on her final journey to merge with something bigger than herself. She had started her journey from the cold and frozen recesses of a glacier, fell thousands of feet over unforgiving rocks, made her way through treacherous ravines and dark jungles, but never lost hope, even as she yearned to be with her true love—the ocean! The sharp edges of the hardest rocks eventually became smooth and soft because of the persistent pursuit of her final abode. Now her joy was boundless as the divine reunion was just around the corner. Soon, she would lose herself completely in the depth and vastness of the ocean and reach the tranquil depths of its bosom. Along this journey, despite the rigors, she had given selflessly to any and all. She had quenched the thirst of the weary traveler, sacrificed herself to the clouds, and supported all forms of life. She had stayed pure to her core, and nothing could make her dirty. Even the mud in her was along only for the journey, as it would also find a resting place in the depths of the ocean leaving nothing but clear and pure water. I sat there motionless absorbing the truth and the beauty of the river's message.

It was then that I realized the true definition of love and of living. The rain had stopped, but my tears of joy were unstoppable. It was as if God had revealed Himself to me.

While religion offers us solace and comfort, many still ache for an original understanding that is not borrowed from well-meaning protectors of faith. Now I had my own version of what it felt like to touch one's own soul. The river is the perfect embodiment of selfless, humble, compassionate love—a love full of life and full of song. Songs of love that we all yearn for and lyrics that make our heart ache with sweet joy. Such love is indeed possible. This realization sent me a wave of joy similar to the one I had felt during my childhood days especially while playing the *manjeeras* (small brass cymbals) in the gurudwara or when serving cold, fragrant water to worshippers during India's summer heat.

That day marked a turning point in my life as I found inspirations everywhere, in the simplest of nature's creations. What seemed ordinary and mundane before became extraordinary and exhilarating. Flowers, trees, butterflies, rustling leaves, the hide-and-seek play of the sun and clouds, starry nights, and moonlight dancing on the waves, among many other natural "wonders" started giving me messages that were uplifting and strangely calming. I started noticing a different beauty in everything around me. I started expressing my exhilaration in 140-character messages online. My younger daughter, Nikita, was my first follower on Twitter. She still chides me on my Confucius-like shift in persona. *"Why are you like this, Dad?"* became her constant refrain. Although, I do believe she secretly liked reading the tweets, but it was just not cool for a teenager to admit as much, especially to her old man.

What I realized was that once we begin discovering the beauty within and without, love is no longer a feeling. Love becomes a way of life. It carves the path for us to live joyously. Despite the clarity and conviction of this realization, the daily din of life can still be a constant struggle, especially in the face of personal challenges. In those difficult hours, Rabindranath Tagore, an Indian poet and mystic, helps soothe my worry through the beautiful collection of his short philosophical inspirations in his book *Stray Birds*. In one entry, he writes, *"The waterfall sings, I find my song, when I find my freedom."* The waterfall sings, even as it sacrifices itself over unforgiving rocks to continue its joyful journey as a river. She is filled with love and a longing for the eternal union with her lover—the ocean—despite the many obstacles she encounters along her journey. And this union is something to behold—peaceful and graceful. One can hear the gratitude of both partners in their silent song as they merge and express timeless love for each other. In Goethe's words, "To witness two lovers is a spectacle for the gods."

It was clear that with time gratitude for the gift of this precious life would begin to enrich me, even if fear and uncertainty is everywhere. I became more introspective, and the yearning to find the true love, our Creator, became stronger and, at times, completely overwhelming. Just the thought of meeting Him stirred feelings of yearning and of being in love. Yes, I can be in love once again—an eternal love that does not fade with time. Perhaps just the seed of this divine love will be enough for me, I thought. The seed, once planted in the heart, will germinate slowly in the warmth of gratitude and compassion. In order for this seed to grow, however, I would have to discard the toxic environment inside me—my duality, the personal narratives of self-pity, and the lies I was telling myself and to those I loved dearly. I needed to become authentic and pure like the river so self-love could seep into my depths also. Compassion would then become the nourishment for this seed to grow roots and sprout life. This poem by Rabindranath Tagore beautifully sums up the emotions I felt as the yearning for true love of the Creator started to take hold inside my heart:

That I want You, only You — let my heart repeat without end. All desires that distract me, day and night, are false and empty to the core.

As the night keeps hidden in its gloom the petition for light, even thus in the depth of my unconsciousness rings the cry "I want You, only You."

As the storm still seeks its end in peace when it strikes against peace with all its might, even thus my rebellion strikes against Your love and still its cry is "I want You, only You."

Such love has the power to truly fulfill us, I realized. Until then the reality is different. Isn't it strange that when we have everything, sometimes it feels like we have nothing at all? Inside we feel like beggars seeking peace when our outer world appears perfectly rich to friends and family. We may have intelligent and beautiful children, a perfect life partner, a gorgeous home in an upscale neighborhood, a thriving career, many amazing friends, all the earthly comforts, and yet we feel empty inside—like a musical instrument that makes beautiful music but is hollow inside. We grope in the dark to search for answers, and we come up empty-handed.

For many years, I went through the same phase of emptiness and questioning all the definitions of happiness that are so familiar to many others. Ironically, in order to counter the emptiness of my soul, all questions led to the same answer—to empty my mind. So, I started meditating and reading philosophical, introspective works to find clues to attain such a peaceful state. Early morning walks brought some relief through walking meditations and introspection. But durable peace remained elusive, and it was difficult to still the mind.

During this search for answers, I came across a translation of *Japji Sahib,* the first scripture of the Sikhs, which dated back to 1974. The translator was one of the most controversial mystics from India—Rajneesh—popularly known as Osho. I was mesmerized by his uncommon wisdom, deep insight, and a refreshing viewpoint that challenged the concepts of morality, organized religion, and society, as we know it. Surprisingly, my wife was equally captivated by his discourses, and we constantly listened to them every time we would get in our respective cars. His ideas made perfect sense, even though some seemed a bit radical. Every time I disagreed with him, I was reminded of my mother's advice that we should be like honeybees—accept the nectar from all flowers, even if they grow among thorns or in dirt and fly away without making a fuss.

Osho's words of wisdom, like the incident on the banks of the river in Costa Rica, became another watershed moment that gave me hope. He opened my mind to viewpoints, ideologies, and opinions that had been shunned by organized religion all my life. Perhaps what I considered sins were definitions created by the religious guard to preserve their own religion, I thought. Fear is a big motivator, and it is no wonder that many in organized religion use the concept of fear in different ways to preserve their faith. I am not against organized religion. In fact, I belonged to one for most of my life. As I have grown spiritually, I have come to believe that one needs to create one's own worldview based on personal experiences rather than accepting the sermons as the ultimate truth. After all, even the religious leaders, as good and well intentioned they may be, are limited by their own personal interpretations of the scriptures. These sermons can be excellent catalysts to unleash our original thought and to help grow our own spiritual wings.

My thirst for knowledge kept increasing, and the bookshelves were soon filled with works authored by Lao Tzu, Rabindranath Tagore, Sri Swami Satchidananda, Mikhail Naimy, Marcus Aurelius, Seneca, Thich Nhat Hanh, Dalai Lama, Khalil Gibran and contemporaries like Dr. Wayne Dyer, Dr. Deepak

Chopra, and Robin Sharma. I learned Transcendental Meditation and became Osho's *sanyasin* (disciple) at a three-day meditation retreat and acquired almost all of his significant works. Meditation brought peace and tranquility, albeit briefly, like nothing else could. I began to grow spiritually in a way that was liberating and fortifying at the same time. Concurrently, the cracks in my marriage were becoming far too big, and our daughters had taken notice. My wife knew me well and instinctively grasped my mental constructs and conflicts. My mother's passing had caused me to reassess my life, its purpose, and mortality itself. In a way, her death was the catalyst that triggered the unzipping of the traumas of the past in the guise of my search for answers. I thought, naively, that knowledge through reading, meditating, and attending mindfulness conferences might lead me to some answers. I felt alone even when surrounded by people who loved me. I could not offer the love and caring that my wife deserved. How could I give her what I did not possess?

Seers like Sri Patanjali, Guru Nanak and others had already suggested that knowledge would not lead to wisdom. "Thoughts would get in the way of silence and peace," is the mantra that several schools of meditation agreed upon. Ironically, I would have to give up my quest for knowledge and abandon all my questions if I wanted the real answers. Silence inside would reveal the answers to all questions. In fact, with silence, all questions would cease because an answer to one question only leads to an unending stream of more questions.

During one of those silent meditations in January 2016, an awareness came out of nowhere. It was as if someone had flipped a light switch … just like a flash of lightning that lights up a fire in the forest. This light revealed an understanding that sent an electric current through my body. It was exhilarating! I began understanding human feelings and emotions like anger, anxiety, depression, and even sexual abuse with a fresh perspective. It all made perfect sense. How could such a simple insight elude me for so long? Just like the soul, it was always there. I had simply placed my knowledge and my ego in the way!

This new insight about the source of suffering and pain has now placed me on a journey of discovery, awareness, and understanding. However, I must submit that this small piece of wisdom and clarity of thought is equally as exciting as it is scary. It's just as lustrous as it is dark. It may help me become more peaceful, but it requires a shift in priorities and the direction of my life's journey. My path will most definitely appear to be selfish to many, especially to those who are closest to me emotionally. That's because it's a journey of the heart and of the soul. It is very personal and intimately internal. I can neither ask anyone to join me, nor can I expect everyone to understand me. As Goethe wrote, "The soul that sees beauty may sometimes walk alone." This journey requires silence of the mind and body—something aloneness offers. Like Osho says, we must first love ourselves with utmost selfishness so that our vessel will be filled to the brim with love. Then, love will have no place to go but overflow to others. Just like misery begets misery, self-love will have the opposite effect. To do this, we need to find our very own Buddha, our own awareness. From Gautama Buddha's wisdom we know that everyone has a Buddha inside—we simply have to awaken him.

2

the awakening

Tears … why are so many afraid of them? Their source is either immense joy or intense sadness—proof that a heart still beats in you.

The word Buddha comes from the root word *budh*, which means to be fully aware. While I can understand this meaning on an intellectual level, it is important for me to feel it in my consciousness if I hope for any transformation. Just like a river's march toward the ocean, much work lies ahead. However, with the newfound awareness described later in this chapter, I believe I can marshal the energies to meet the obstacles I will face on this journey. As I do, I believe the answers to the questions that still plague me will reveal themselves when I least expect them to. And those answers will continue to shift my life in many profound ways.

Perhaps most profound of all, I believe that this new awareness will support the idea that the path to *the Way* or lasting peace, which Lao Tzu explained so eloquently in the *Tao Te*

Ching, is inside us. But how do we reach those depths where this secret is revealed? I believe that we can attain such depths through the altruistic acts of helping other souls find *their* Light. And, in return, we will find our own. With selfless compassion, we can help others remove the darkness from their life. The simple act of witnessing the gradual removal of this darkness will fill our soul also with the divine Light and true happiness. It is not surprising that Buddha, Guru Nanak, Rabindranath Tagore, Zarathustra, Lao Tzu, and every other enlightened soul and mystic preached service, compassion, and humility. I believe they were giving us clues all along so we could end our suffering without engaging in drastic actions like becoming an ascetic. This simple answer has been in front of us all this time, but its evidence lies in the experience of this truth in our daily life. What's needed is a conscious awareness of the pleasure that selfless giving brings to our soul.

Consider a common example of giving someone a thoughtful gift. How does it feel when that gift is truly appreciated and you can see genuine gratitude in the eyes, words, and actions of the recipient? You will agree that a mystical joy and sense of happiness flows through every fiber of our being. Buddhists call this form of joy *mudita* or sympathetic joy or altruistic joy. Thich Nhat Hanh, a renowned Vietnamese Buddhist monk, poet, and peacemaker goes one step further in his book *The Heart of the*

Buddha's Teaching since he considers these definitions of *mudita* too limiting. He believes that "a deeper definition of *mudita* is joy that is filled with peace and contentment." Isn't this the same joy that we are all seeking? A joy that makes us feel good about life. A joy akin to the kind Buddha must have felt when he achieved *nirvana* or enlightenment.

So, if giving a simple gift of happiness to others brings us so much peace and joy, imagine what a gift of healing someone would do for our soul. It could be life-changing, for both the recipient and the giver. Helping others makes us feel better about ourselves, period! Whether it is sponsoring an orphan to support her education or working in the soup kitchen to feed the homeless, altruism fills us with joy, peace and contentment especially when we don't desire anything in return. Because *mudita* is in our innate nature, it is immensely gratifying to the soul. The path or the Way that will fill us with gratitude and lead us toward lasting peace passes through the humble valley of service to others. If the answer is so simple and so barrenly laid in front of us, then what's keeping us from being joyful and is making the human condition miserable? I call it The Gap— explained in greater detail in the next chapter.

The Gap signifies the divide between a two-faced life and authentic living, the separation between darkness and Light, the space between suffering and peace. This is the chasm that we must fill with Light so that we can clearly see our original soul - the innocent soul from which we were separated at birth. An understanding of the genesis of The Gap could fill us with the desire to remove someone's pain and suffering, or karunā, the Sanskrit word that Buddha used to explain this expression of compassion. Then we could begin to have a compassionate appreciation for not only the human emotions and states of being like anger, despair, anxiety, fear, humility, gratitude, and happiness but also human behavior and reactions to events like infidelity, divorce, sexual abuse, and severe emotional trauma.

Such an appreciation could then provide a deeper insight into the first two of the Four Noble Truths that Buddha preached—that there is suffering, and that there is a path or source of suffering. Knowing what causes the suffering is half the battle in pursuit of lasting peace because once we know the source of suffering, then there's hope of finding the path to end it. In the field of medicine, ancient or modern, a doctor must first know and understand what's causing an illness before prescribing a course of action that would relieve the patient of pain and suffering. Often the prescription for the same ailment differs from one patient to another based on the doctor's expert understanding of the treatment that may produce the best results. This applies not just to physical illness but also to mental ailments. A psychologist or psychiatrist will spend hours probing into a person's life before designing a treatment regimen.

Doctors and psychologists can help but only up to a point since they are dealing with physical matter—the brain. If we can tap into our tranquil depths, we can transcend the physical and touch the subtle and the nuanced—our Inner Self. Then we can be our own doctors and our own refuge, as Buddha preached. If we can diagnose the source of our pain, we can then begin the work to end it without external aids or band aids that treat only the symptoms. We can remove the root cause of our suffering … forever!

While suffering is very personal, how we experience it is uniquely shaped by many sociocultural and religious factors. From a very early age, the concepts of sin, guilt, pity and shame begin to get defined by our environment and the lens through which we see the world. Trauma and abuse, if experienced early in childhood, fractures our soul in ways that are difficult to comprehend even by many well trained psychologists. Regardless, the narratives we build in our heads have common threads that are all too familiar to anyone who has experienced any form of trauma, physical pain, or emotional suffering – narratives of guilt, shame, self-pity, anger, despair, helplessness, anxiety, and depression plague us and sometimes overwhelm the ability to function normally. To be sure, such suffering is not new. It dates back to the very beginning of mankind.

Adam's suffering began after he ate of the Forbidden Fruit and duality entered his being. Now good and bad, hot and cold, happy and sad became harsh realities for him. Life for Adam had changed forever. Gautama Buddha pronounced the Four Noble Truths about suffering over 2,500 years ago. In his first sermon in Deer Park in the city of Sarnath, India, Buddha explained to his first five disciples that all human beings, without any exception, experience suffering of some kind. He further clarified that there were clear reasons or sources that cause suffering. Buddha offered hope in the Third Noble Truth that the suffering can cease and that sentient beings can find peace and joy. Through his personal experience, he declared in the Fourth Noble Truth that suffering can end if we can rid ourselves of all ill will, all desires, and our ignorance. Even though we may be able to remove ill will and ignorance, removal of all desires is a tall order for most of us. Our brains have been wired since birth to teach us that desires are good since they lead us to "happiness."

Life would have been so much easier if he had also provided three simple do-it-yourself steps to end our suffering! The Eightfold Path that Buddha prescribed, if followed in disciplined manner for a long time, can be transformational. However, some associate that with being a Buddhist and, therefore, it does not have universal appeal. I was seeking an answer that was simple in application, non-religious, deeply human and universal. Something that Buddha and all other enlightened beings agreed upon. A golden nugget that was part of our innate nature and did not create any conflict with other parts of our life.

Almost every religion has examined suffering albeit from a different vantage point. For example, Guru Nanak, the first guru of the Sikh religion, proclaimed *"Nanak dukhiya sab sansaar,"* meaning "Oh Nanak, the entire world is afflicted with pain." Unjustified suffering of the innocent is integral to Christianity, as the Bible's entire Book of Job is dedicated to this question, and this issue is also covered at great length in both the Old and New Testaments. Hinduism, like Buddhism, uses the words *dukkha* and *kleshas* to describe the physical, mental, and emotional instability and afflictions in the material world or *samsara*. Hindus, like Buddhists, believe suffering is an inescapable part of a human being's journey, for as long as the illusion of the transient material objects and sensual pleasures keep us entangled. Hindus call this illusory world maya. Acceptance of pain as a reality of life is also central to Hindus, as it helps relieve some of the pain and suffering by making us stronger—akin to gold going through fire to become a beautiful ornament. Some equate such acceptance of pain with surrender, as in surrendering to God and His plan for us in this mortal life. The implication of such surrender is that while the physical body may suffer, our inner self is indestructible as explained in the *Bhagavad Gita,* the sacred scripture of the Hindus.

Jainism, a religion that coexisted with Buddhism, considers karmā, or our actions, as the cause of suffering. Jains also believe in the concept of nirvana, or liberation from the cycle of birth and death, by following an austere and disciplined life. Suffering in Islam, however, is more literal and physical rather than conceptual. For example, there are three types of suffering in Islam: suffering caused by our own negligence; suffering caused by natural disasters; and suffering caused by other persons, such as tyrant rulers. Finally, Zoroastrianism, one of the world's most ancient religions, believes in the existence of evil that leads us to sin. While Zoroastrianism doesn't address the concept of suffering directly, the precepts are very similar to other religions like Buddhism, Christianity, and Hinduism, especially in the belief that sins can be eradicated by our own right actions. A whole chapter in this book is dedicated to the concept of sin and how it relates to suffering.

Regardless of the religion we affiliate ourselves with, there are some common behaviors and societal expectations that transcend geography and cultures. For example, in most parts of the world, showing too much emotion is a sign of weakness for a "real" man. This belief applies even to presidential candidates, who can win or lose an election based on how their strength is perceived by the populace. One tear at the wrong moment and the chances of becoming president can drown in it. Even as a common citizen, we cannot seem to escape such an expectation. For many years, I could only express the depth of my loss and suffering in private. Frankly, after my father's suicide, there was little time to deal with the enormity of the loss. Despite many years of toil and hard work, my father was unable to secure a financial future for the family. Therefore, we had real financial distress building underneath the surface. So, I did what real men are supposed to do—I became a caretaker for the family as best as I could.

While our narratives have common themes, I am limited in my understanding of suffering by my own experiences and my interpretations of events that I label as painful. To explore this topic further, I had to come to terms with my own vulnerability. I believe that doing so gave me enormous inner strength. Exposing our wounds takes courage, but doing that in an honest manner can allow them to heal in an environment of authenticity. Nothing has been more liberating for me than authenticity. Dr. Brené Brown, an author and researcher of human guilt, shame, and vulnerability at the University of Houston, agrees and speaks extensively about this subject in her inspirational work titled *The*

Power of Vulnerability. Every time I hear her explanation of vulnerability, I am overwhelmed with hope and self-love. She says, "Vulnerability is the birthplace of love, belonging, joy, courage, empathy, and creativity. It is the source of hope, empathy, accountability, and authenticity. If we want greater clarity in our purpose or deeper and more meaningful spiritual lives, vulnerability is the path." I encourage you to put faith in her statement and you will discover the rewards quickly. I surely did.

One aspect of vulnerability is to face your own "demons." My biggest demon was the guilt and shame attached to some of my actions over the years that I labeled as sinful. The construct of sin that I had learned as a child is the one closely related to the Sanskrit word karmā or one's conscious deeds. Good karmā or behavior led one to "heaven" while bad karmā was a sure pathway to "hell." This was the assumption of my organized religion. I was becoming more cynical of such assumptions because they failed to provide logical answers. The quest to find some explanations continued and almost consumed me day and night. Readings led to meditations, attendance at mindfulness conferences and gatherings, introspections, early morning walking meditations, and prayers. But the turmoil inside me did not calm down for decades.

Then on a warm day in January 2016 in Florida everything changed. During an unusually deep meditation, my mantra (a sacred utterance) was mystically replaced by the chant of karunā, perhaps because all my readings about Buddha's wisdom were imbued with compassion. I found myself in a dark cave, and I could hear what sounded like celestial music, even as echoes of karunā surrounded me. I had been in this cave before in one of my childhood dreams. In those dreams, the cave had cold water flowing over my feet, and dimly lit figures of deities were spread out all over among dark, wet, and ragged, rocky openings, except they were alive. Now they were gone and it was a desolate and scary place.

The music was replaced by what initially sounded like someone sobbing. The sobs grew into painful wails, and hundreds of floating shadows in human form appeared out of nowhere. The chant of "karunā ... karunā ... karunā" echoed everywhere. The shadows were wearing a white garb that was covering their heads. They had no faces—just darkness in its place—and only busts that were floating in midair. These shadows were taking turns and placing young children wrapped in white blankets in my lap as the wails became more intense. These children seemed to be very sick. Their bodies shook with sobs as if their cries had sapped all energy from their small, fragile bodies. As I looked down at them, their plight overwhelmed me, and my tears fell on their soft cheeks. I embraced these children and felt a sense of calm I had never experienced before. Even though my body felt ablaze with energy, I felt strangely but immensely serene. The shadows kept taking the children from my lap and then dissolved into the darkness until the last one was gone. The soft echoes of karunā continued, and I was enveloped in a quality of peace and serenity that I had never experienced before.

Then like a flash of unanticipated lightning, a small spark of awareness touched my soul. I was back in the dark cave alone, and I was sobbing incessantly.

I came out of the meditation with that last vision. I was completely shaken by this experience, as I could still feel the energy and the presence of the shadows all around me. I slowly opened my eyes and found myself still sitting in front of the tall Buddha statue that was dimly lit from behind. I looked at the clock, and over an hour had elapsed. This was unusual, as my normal meditations ended after about twenty minutes. The alarm that I normally used to end my meditation had not gone off. Maybe I had not turned on the alarm or I had switched it off after it was activated. It didn't matter. I decided to go for a walk to get some fresh air.

As I stepped outside, the whole world around me seemed different. I did not know what was happening, and I remember being afraid and strangely peaceful at the same time. I walked gazing at the trees and hearing the birds as if experiencing them for the first time. The sun was setting in the horizon, and the sky was ablaze with color. A soft, cool breeze was moving through the trees, and the leaves were dancing in synchrony. Everything seemed to be moving in slow motion. Every sound was musical, and every movement in nature was like a well-choreographed dance. It was as if I was floating through space—everything I was experiencing was in me, and I was in everything else around me. I stopped at a restaurant to get a drink of water just to be sure that this wasn't a dream state.

My mind was racing through all kinds of thoughts that were simply out of the ordinary realm of my experience. The spark had lit a raging fire inside me, and insights kept pouring in like I was drinking from a fire hose. I increased my pace to return home and began writing—my maiden effort to capture all that I was feeling and beginning to understand. The result is the book that's in your hands.

Mysteriously but with uncommon clarity, I now understood that suffering begins when we are separated from our mother's womb, our Creator, at birth; the material world (maya) is *not* the source of suffering but only an object of our desires. It is our *insatiable craving* for the material and sensual pleasures that causes the pain and steeps us in darkness. Buddha's Fourth Noble Truth confirms the same fact but I now had an understanding of the source of this yearning. Cravings for maya, as misguided and fruitless as they may be, arise in us for a very special and almost divine reason—to be as joyful and peaceful as we were when we were united with our Higher Self in our mother's womb. Now I knew how to access the inner wisdom to end the suffering caused by these cravings. The answer lies bare in our actions; in our selfless compassion for those innocent souls whose pain is just as real as our own. All they need is a compassionate helping hand to help heal their scars. As we serve them selflessly and witness the removal of their darkness, we begin to find our Light also. Karunā alone holds the power for this internal transformation.

This awareness became the foundation for this book, and as you read this book, your personal knowledge may be affected in the following ways:

First, you may recognize that all human conditions, positive or negative, are manifestations of our desire to be peaceful and joyful. Therefore, all our states of being, whether evil or kind, moral or immoral, good or bad, have their genesis in something pure and divine—our yearning to be reunited with our Inner Self where eternal happiness lives.

Second, you may appreciate that the traditional view that informs our understanding of the human condition can be viewed differently through the lens of compassion I call *We are Human!* or *The Wah! Perspective. Wah!*, coincidentally, is an expression of pleasure, appreciation, surprise, wonder, and praise in Hindi and

Urdu languages and is used as a prefix before the beginning of several words and sentences or on its own as an exclamation. When used repeatedly (*Wah! Wah! Wah!*) it expresses exuberant praise and joy generally during live music concerts or poetry performances. Sikhs use the word Wah-Guru or Waheguru to signify the sense of wonder on God's creation, to express happiness, and even consolation or condolence.

Finally, you may reach the same conclusion as the one I reached that the original source of our suffering is the same regardless of whether it manifests itself physically or mentally or emotionally. It's our separation from the Creator at birth.

To be sure, this "lens" is not a new invention. It most certainly is not my original idea. It has existed for as long as enlightened souls have walked the earth. All of them, from Jesus to Guru Nanak, and our contemporary spiritual teachers, philanthropists, and others have provided clues that lead to the same path. Perhaps what's different is how it has affected me and has shaped my view about human conditions like anger, anxiety, suicide, and sin, among others. I believe the seeds of this awakening were sown many years ago during a stormy day in Costa Rica.

I am neither a trained psychologist nor an experienced mystic. I am certainly not an ascetic who has been roaming the jungles or the Himalayas, and I do not claim to be an enlightened soul. I am a mortal human being, complete with vulnerabilities and frailties, engaged in living life with all its trials, tribulations, joys, and sorrows. I am also a seeker just like many of you looking for answers to questions that have plagued us for decades. Meditation, introspection, and concentration have unveiled what I believe is the source of common suffering and the present human condition. It's The Gap—fortunately, as you will discover later, this is also where suffering can end.

3

birth of The Gap

Answers lead us into a state of ego; mystery leads us into a state of wonder; curiosity leads us to inner growth through understanding.

My older daughter's birth was not an easy one, to put it lightly. After twenty-seven long hours of labor, she literally had to be wrestled with and pulled out with a vacuum. As gorgeous as she was at almost ten pounds, she had a conical head, a dislocated shoulder, a bruised forehead, and she was not breathing when she came out of her mother's womb. I almost fainted. The doctors held her upside down and patted her butt and back, used a tube to suck out stuff from her throat before she bellowed out a huge cry. She had huge lungs; she still does! I almost fainted again. She was born on her own terms. I knew then that she was going to be a strong-headed child who will lead her life on her own schedule. Of course, everyone around her, including the nurses and doctors, was completely overwhelmed with joy. I am convinced that my wife forgot all her pain, albeit for a few moments, associated with such a traumatic first childbirth experience. We named her Neha, meaning love.

As Neha cried, tears of joy filled the room. Nurses explained that Neha was simply shocked by the sharp sounds, strange surroundings, bright lights, and the cold air hitting her body. They must have been right, as she stopped crying after she was wrapped in warm blankets and placed gently in her proud mother's arms. Neha's eyes locked with her mother's, and they communicated oceans of divine love through that simple gaze. It is true—one never forgets the birth of the first child.

It is a well-regarded fact that birth is one of, if not, the most traumatic experience in the life of a human being. The mother's womb is one of those comforting places where there are no harsh sounds, no blinding lights, no jarring disturbances, and there is no need to expend any effort to breathe or eat because the mother does that for the baby. It's nine months of silent meditation—like *Vipassana* mindfulness meditation. (*Vipassana* means *seeing things as they really are* and is a meditative technique first taught by Buddha.) Some believe that we actually dream about our previous lives and commune with our Creator while we are comfortably doubled over in the womb. It's perhaps the most peaceful position for a human being. Even as adults, we still find the fetal position to be one of the most comforting ways to find peace, solace, and even sleep, especially during times of distress and anxiety. When we are cold, we find warmth in the fetal position, almost naturally. These natural impulses cannot be a coincidence.

At the time of natural birth, the baby is squeezed through the narrow dark birth canal, sometimes with the assistance of a vacuum tube or metal forceps. As soon as the baby comes out of the mother's womb, an unfamiliar environment greets her. She takes her first breath, and the very first exhalation is a huge cry of discomfort and pain as if she is saying, "Oh please, please, please! Please put me back in the warmth of the womb. Why are you doing this to me? Why are you disturbing my meditative sleep? Are you out of your mind that you are patting my back and butt so I can breathe? I was breathing just fine inside. See what you have done to my head? I look like a freak with a cone head! And why are you cutting off my food and air supply? That's the umbilical cord, you stupid fellows! And you call yourselves doctors? Any of you strange figures, can you please help me? Please put me back where I belong, with my Creator. Oh please, someone help me!"

Weighing machines, measuring tools, smiles, tears of joy, camera flashes, and celebrations answer her wailing pleas. Within moments, her peaceful world is shattered forever and she is permanently separated from the mother as the umbilical cord is cut—a real and somewhat ironical metaphor for the severing of her connection with her mother, her Creator, so she can survive independently. The Gap is thus born, albeit a small one at this time.

This Gap is a small but significant separation of the newborn from her innocent soul, her Higher Self, her Creator, her mother. She cries not because of the strange environment she witnesses at birth but because of the trauma of this separation. Her world of meditative peace, where she was one with her soul, is forever changed, and she desperately wants it to be the way it was for the first nine months of her life. She wants to reach and touch her Creator but The Gap separating her from her innocent soul is already too big for her little hands. Anyone would cry uncontrollably if her world were altered permanently and so drastically. The pain is real and the anguish is indelibly impressed upon the innocent mind—forming a crack, a separation from her Creator, her soul, her Inner Self.

Dr. Lisa Miller, the creative inspiration and force behind the Spirituality Mind Body Institute at Teachers College and Professor of Psychology and Education at Columbia University, in her book *The Spiritual Child,* convincingly argues that we are genetically hardwired for spirituality. In other words, we are born with an inner sense of a connection with a higher power. Spirituality is inherent and genetically present in us. What's even more remarkable is that most, if not all of us, are very aware of it—just like our sense of touch, taste, and smell. It is not too farfetched then to infer that the pain we feel at the severing of the spiritual connection is real and emotionally jarring for the innocent child. But because spirituality is innate and cannot be extricated, it is, therefore, also reasonable to assume that The Gap or feeling of separation from our Creator is merely an illusion. We cannot be separated from this higher power, even if we try because spirituality is biologically inherent. The Creator is, in fact, our spirit, our soul, our Inner Self, our Higher Self, and is always an inseparable part of our being. The illusion of this separation, however, seems very real and becomes stronger with each passing day until it starts to feel real.

The painful desire we experience when we come out of our mother's womb is of the simplest and purest form—the desire to be one with our Creator, the desire to be at peace, the desire to return to our mother's womb. To ease our pain during childhood, our well-meaning caretakers fill our lives with rattles, toys, games, clothes and the like to keep us "happy." As we grow older, we are sold the "package" that if we behave in a way that our society considers normal and honorable, then happiness will follow. Getting a good education, developing proper etiquette, getting married, having kids, being responsible parents, and then grandparents all become part of the recipe to achieve happiness in life. We buy into this model enthusiastically. It seems real because we can see it, hear it, touch it, smell it, and even taste it.

Everyone is doing it, so we come to believe that it must be true. Because material comforts awaken all five senses, it is natural for an innocent child and a young adult to believe that this happiness will eventually be real.

The innocence that stays with us until about three or four years of age keeps fading until we are ready to take on the real world and start the first day of school. Up until that time, we were fearless, spontaneous, and filled with unstoppable and infectious laughter. We were full of intrigue, captivated by a fluttering butterfly or a rainbow, and the simplest things gave us immense pleasure. We were present in the moment. Then one day we are dressed up in our best clothes to attend the first day of school. Uncontrollable crying generally marks this "happy" day. The separation from our parents torments us because it is a painful reminder of the day we were born, when we were separated from our mother, our Inner Self. It's déjà vu all over again. We are being removed from our parents, our world, our toys, our comfortable high chair, our Cheerios, and our familiar surroundings. And our parents are celebrating once again with smiles and camera flashes. Tears well up because our consciousness remembers how we were similarly removed from the comfort of her mother's womb and cut off from our Creator. Tears are joined by cries for help to stop this separation. We try to hold on to our Creator, our parent, only to see our keeper, our protector's figure turn into a shadow and eventually vanish into the distance. The image of the Creator becomes faint yet again. The damage is done and The Gap widens as a new layer of disappointment and darkness veils the view of our Inner Self.

Psychologists call it separation anxiety—an emotional reaction the child suffers when she is separated from her parents. It's not new, however. It's the reemergence of the emotional scar of separation that was created at birth. This type of anxiety is most common in preschoolers, who are yet to develop a sense of self. Even as adults, some of us feel it when we leave home for college or leave our hometown, our family for a new job in a different town, or when we migrate to a different country. It's more pronounced and starkly visible in preschoolers because they still have some of the innocence and, therefore, a connection, albeit fragile and faint, with the Creator.

This process of repeatedly being displaced from our comfort zone into a strange environment is what we call change. It is embedded in our consciousness from birth. Is it any wonder that most of us are afraid of change, even though it is as natural as our skin changing and renewing itself every so often? In fact, for some, change can create unusual anxiety and cause panic attacks. If a baby could explain this at birth, I am convinced psychologists would call the baby's wails nothing short of severe anxiety and a panic attack induced by a dramatic change of circumstance. Psychologists and social scientists ascribe a variety of theories to the concept of change and the human reaction to it. Perhaps the answer lies in the fact that our consciousness never forgets the first experience of life-altering change at birth and the formation of the crack that separated us from our innocent soul, our Inner Being. We desperately want to reunite with our peaceful abode, but we are frustrated in our attempts as that goal continues to elude us.

It is common human behavior to rigorously chase the things that evade us especially if we believe they will bring us happiness. Over time, this craving for happiness and lasting peace becomes the central theme of our life and it keeps getting stronger. Our futile attempts at finding the original serenity only bring pain and suffering. As Buddha pronounced, our life will be filled with suffering unless we can find a way to reunite with our Creator. That's our quest, except we mistakenly think that the Creator is hiding behind the material things. It's really not our fault. Our caretakers conditioned us for this response. It's not the fault of the caretakers either because they were exposed to the same beliefs.

Buddha considers the desire and craving for the material world as one of the root causes of suffering. The question that always arose in me was about the source of this craving—where does it come from? The earliest time we could have developed such a desire is at birth, when our caretakers first introduced us to maya, the Hindu and Buddhist word signifying illusion of this phenomenal world. However, for the innocent infant this is not a desire in the way we adults know and understand it—the desire to accumulate material success, sensual pleasures, societal honor, fame, and other impermanent things. The new, innocent life hasn't been exposed to this maya in any significant way just yet. Her craving is to return to the peaceful state in the womb.

Unfortunately, maya is the only visible and tangible source of fulfillment and relief after birth. As we grow older, we begin to associate relief—from hunger, low position in society, bills, sexual urges, and other stressors of life—with happiness. Desires keep increasing because there's a positive feedback loop of acquiring worldly things and the resulting experience of relief. It is natural, therefore, to reach the conclusion that a lot of maya must bring a much higher level of satisfaction and relief, a fleeting form of happiness. What we are seeking, albeit in material and sensual pleasures, is still the original happiness and peace we felt in our mother's womb. It's the same desire we had at birth—to find the joy and fulfillment that comes from being one with our Inner Self. Just like the meditation and silence that calmed us in our mother's womb, we begin to believe that maya will have the same effect. After all, the experienced caretakers, educators, and others in society who *appear* to be happy must know better. This becomes one of our earliest belief systems.

What we experience, though, is only transitory pleasure in the form of relief. Just like the impermanent and illusory maya, true happiness also starts feeling the same—temporary and fleeting. Small events trigger a small dose of joy, and soon unhappiness, anger, anxiety, and other human conditions follow. Even as we realize this fact, we find it hard to extricate ourselves from the confusing jumble and web of material pleasures precisely because the passing feelings of happiness they bring are now hardwired in the pleasure centers of our brains. We want to reach the true source of happiness, but we don't know any other way except the path that leads to more of the same. The greed and the lust for material comforts, sensual pleasure, power, and position continues to magnify and intensify our suffering as we begin to realize that the ultimate goal of finding our Higher Self continues to remain as elusive as ever. The layers of mortal desires fill The Gap with darkness and, unaware of what's happening to us, we start becoming removed from our own Light. In cultures that place emphasis on individuality and independence from a very early age, *The Gap* starts to widen and begins to fill with darkness much earlier in life. It's no surprise, therefore, that we find so many teenagers trapped in the web of addictions. All they want is peace and happiness, but they seek it through external numbing traps instead of inner awareness. Psychedelic drugs like magic mushrooms, ayahuasca, LSD, and others have skyrocketed in popularity over the last few decades because they create feelings of immense joy. Users report "spiritual experiences" of transcending space and time. Such drugs create their own temporary reality of unbound freedom and peace, and they become addictive because it is those exact feelings that our soul has sought since birth. However, our innocence gets lost somewhere along the way.

The Gap, therefore, has its genesis at birth and, as we grow older, it continues to pervade our entire mortal life accumulating layers of darkness. There are only two states of being where The Gap does not exist, or if it does, it is completely filled with the Light—in a baby when she is in the womb, or in an enlightened soul. Both are closest to the Creator. We accept this as the truth when we think of enlightened souls. But to believe that a baby is enlightened in her own way is a bit of a stretch. However, we don't have to look far for evidence that little children are also close to the pure, peaceful, and joyful soul. We experience this proof almost every day, but we are simply not aware of it. Just watch the interaction between an adult and a child, even when they are strangers to each other. Is it any wonder that old and young alike break into smiles when they see a baby? They try to engage her gaze and make her smile by making funny faces, sticking the tongue out, waving hands, making childish noises, and the like. We notice this exchange everywhere—in public places, in buses, trains, airports, parties, and kindergartens. And when that baby smiles, there's a strange joy and peace that we experience. That's because a baby's smiling eyes are filled with purity and innocence. Our consciousness recognizes something simple yet powerful in that smile—our Creator. It reminds us of our own innocence and the connection we once had with our Creator.

The Gap was not as wide when we were little children; when we were full of life—fearless, joyful, peaceful. We, as adults, continue to have an innate desire to return to that innocence— we want to be happy. And we feel an even stronger pull when our eyes lock with those of a baby and she smiles. It sends a wave of warmth, peace, and joy through our body, even when we have no blood relation to this child. We don't even know her name, her family, or anything else about her. It is simply our thirst and aching desire to reunite with our Creator that draws us to the innocence of a child. We witness the Creator through the Light in the child's eyes.

We don't engage in this behavior with adolescents, teenagers, or adults. Why is that? Aren't the older ones human beings? Aren't they the embodiment of our Creator? Are we afraid that they may not smile back or that we may look silly making all those strange faces? We may not actively think about it, but our consciousness knows the answer. It's all about The Gap! The layers of darkness that have settled in The Gap over the years in an older human being have pushed the image of our soul, our Creator, farther into the distance. Maya has clouded the view. We know intuitively that we cannot find in an older human being what we can easily capture from a child's gaze. The soft and luminous innocence of truth has become opaque, as we have become filled with worldly knowledge and an insatiable desire to accumulate material pleasures.

Some religions claim that children are an embodiment of God. Many scriptures of organized religion recognize that children are closest to God and implore us to shed our ego and become childlike. For example, Jesus asks his disciples to be childlike if they wish to reach His Kingdom. Buddha suggests the same, and so does Guru Nanak. Dalai Lama's successor is identified when he is still a child. The important question we must ask ourselves is, Why? Perhaps, that line of enquiry will lead us all to a similar conclusion that children represent the embodiment of what's pure, peaceful, fearless, serene, and joyful. Just like the Creator, children represent the soul that we envision and yearn for. A soul that is ever present in us but is difficult to reach because of The Gap. A child's smiling eyes close The Gap, albeit momentarily.

As we grow older and begin our march toward mortality, we fear losing the opportunity to connect with our own innocence that was the source of so much happiness. The flip side of birth is death—the biggest fear of most of mankind. It's not death that we fear; I believe what truly scares us in our subconscious is that we may never unite with our soul, as every passing second is an unstoppable movement toward our own mortality. Hence the urgency to find peace—to find our Creator. To close The Gap and to fill it with Light before death.

The inability to reach our Higher Self manifests itself in a variety of emotions like anger, anxiety, sickness, and depression. At times, these emotions tragically lead to addictions, sexual abuse, and even suicide. It's ironic and tragic that something that is born from a pure desire to find peace and tranquility can lead to so much chaos, pain, and suffering.

But awakened souls like Gautama Buddha, Guru Nanak, Jesus, Mohammed, and numerous others have offered us a simple path that leads us toward Light. They all agree that the biggest culprit that keeps us in the cesspool of suffering is our ego, our own shadow. Ego singlehandedly could be responsible for all the darkness in The Gap. That is because ego is the power behind our strong desire to preserve our being, to remain in control, to assert our presence, to live in the belief that we matter regardless of the fact that we are all mortals. Ego or our sense of self is also responsible for the human conditions that prevent us from witnessing the Light. We are all haunted by our own shadow, our own darkness, our ego.

Mikhail Naimy, a Lebanese author, gives us some sage advice in *The Book of Mirdad* when Micayon and Naronda, two disciples, hold a nocturnal chat with Mirdad, the enlightened soul:

"The shadowless only are in the light. The shadowless only know one God. For God is Light, and Light alone is able to know Light." And he continues as he answers Micayon's request to not speak in riddles:

"All is a riddle to the man who trails a shadow. For that man walks in borrowed light, therefore he stumbles on his shadow. When you become ablaze with Understanding, then shall you cast no shadows any more."

Guru Granth Sahib, the holy scripture of the Sikh religion, offers the same insight that "we find ourselves when we lose ourselves (our ego)." The Sikh gurus, from their own life experiences, suggest that the way to remove our ego from our path toward peace is through humility and through the destruction of the five vices that rob us of our peace—lust, anger, greed, attachment, and hubris. Buddha had offered similar advice over 2,500 years ago. It is hard to love, especially love oneself, if one is filled with hubris and other mortal afflictions. In fact, as we will examine later, when humility is covered with the darkness of hubris, love is simply not possible. Hubris is only concerned with the self while love is the concern for others. Therefore, the two cannot coexist.

Karunā is that universal solvent that dissolves all the dirt and darkness associated with all human conditions and bares the pure soul of each individual. It allows us to recognize that every human expression, regardless of how the observers perceive it, is a desire to experience lasting peace and joy. This is true even for ego and its worst form of mutation—hubris.

4

ego and hubris

A whirlpool of desires can drain you and even drown you. Choose the calm waters—let humility be your sail and contentment your boat.

For as long as I can remember, I have dutifully and respectfully stood in line to offer *sewa,* or service, after the conclusion of the Sunday service at the gurudwara. This *sewa* involved serving prasād or guru's blessing in the form of a warm, delicious halwa—a sweet and delicious rendering of wheat flour roasted in butter. A "true" Sikh, complete with turban, beard, and other adornments, always offers the first five offerings of the prasād to five other "true" Sikhs sitting in the congregation,. This practice honors the five loved ones, or Panj Pyāre, as they were collectively called, who offered their heads as a sacrifice to the tenth Sikh guru, Guru Gobind Singh. From my appearance, I don't look like a true Sikh because I wasn't born in a Sikh family. I was, therefore, never allowed to serve the first five offerings. And it always bothered me. The Sikh gurus preached destruction of all man-made barriers, religious customs, and nonsensical traditions. The Sikh scriptures are filled with rebuke of such practices that create distinctions and discriminations. The Sikh gurus included the writings of even Shudras, or untouchables, in the Holy Scriptures. Every human being was a representation of God, they had stressed. "Na Ko Hindu, Na Ko Mussalmaan," meaning "There's no Hindu, there's no Muslim," were the first words uttered by the first Sikh guru, Guru Nanak Dev Ji, when he emerged enlightened from the river after being missing for three days. This universal acceptance is what appealed so much to me about the Sikh religion. The incredible contradiction during sewa, therefore, made me extremely uncomfortable and somewhat irritated inside.

As I think about it now, it was clearly my sense of self or my ego that was getting bruised every Sunday. The raw wound never got a chance to heal since I hardly ever missed this service because it brought so much peace to my soul. I had proclaimed Guru Nanak as my default father after my dad committed suicide. I sought His advice, and I never left the gurudwara disappointed— the day's hymns and the hukamnama, or the week's guidance offered from the scriptures at the conclusion of the service, always answered my questions. He was my savior, my shelter, and my refuge during good and bad times. So, I quietly swallowed my pride and never said a word to anyone about this conflict in my mind. This is just how it was, and I had to accept this reality despite the fact that it was completely disharmonious with the Sikh gurus' preaching.

However, as I meditated on this question, I realized that it was not just my ego that was becoming an obstacle to peace. It was, in fact, a clash of egos—my own and that of the organized religion—that was creating this friction. The religious guard of almost every religion has created customs of all kinds to create and protect their own identity. In a way, the religious ego is far more rigid than the human ego because it has developed deep roots over tens, if not, hundreds of years. While the human ego is subject to reason and even annihilation through self-actualization, no one would dare dismantle the religious pride. We have all witnessed the extremely destructive societal effects when ego, whether in humans or religions, turns into its more dangerous cousin—hubris. Accounts of narcissists like Adolf Hitler during the Holocaust make our hearts ache, and religious cults where young girls are married to old men in the name of religious service sicken our souls. Such is the power of ego, especially if left unchecked. It turns into a hubris that can leave many casualties in its wake. As history informs us, it almost never ends well, especially for the victim.

Hubris, in the ancient Greek language, had a rather strong sexual connotation, including an implication of sexual abuse. It referred to acts of misdirected pride, and even narcissism, that shamed and humiliated the victim for the pleasure or gratification of the abuser. Hence, hubris, in its ugly form, can be a two-sided saber that shames the perpetrator in his quest for gratification and has a devastating effect on the abused. The definition, however, sheds light on the person possessed with an overwhelming sense of pride. Such a mental construct could result in physical acts that violated laws that in modern times would be equivalent to assault and battery, generally of a sexual or physical nature. Therefore, an accusation of hubris often implied that suffering or punishment would follow.

In more modern times, the proverb "Pride goeth before destruction, a haughty spirit before a fall" (Proverbs 16:18) sums up the rather negative meaning associated with hubris. Proverbs like "The higher you look, the harder you fall" also fit the definition of hubris. Or the Latin proverb "Qui petit alta nimis retro lapsus ponitur imis" meaning "He who aims too high sinks back among the lowest."

Hubris has its foundation in ego, which the Cambridge Dictionary defines as "the idea or opinion that you have of yourself, especially the level of your ability and intelligence, and your importance as a person." Austrian physician Sigmund Freud's most important gift to the world of psychology is the idea that the human psyche has more than one dimension. More precisely, he suggested that human personality has three parts: the id, the ego, and the superego, and that each of them develop at different stages of our lives. In his books *Beyond the Pleasure Principle* and *The Ego and the Id*, Freud provides valuable insights into this trinity of human dimension that's extremely relevant to our discussion of *The Gap*.

According to Freud, the id is the primitive and instinctive component of personality embedded in our unconscious that has a sexual and aggressive side to it. It is a gift of nature that we inherit at birth and operates on the *pleasure principle*, which says that every impulsive desire must be immediately satisfied regardless of the consequences. It is not concerned with the reality of the world around it. Hence, the crying, hungry baby is immediately quieted once it is fed milk. Freud called this behavior *primary process thinking* and considered it to be primitive, illogical, irrational, and fantasy oriented. The personality of the newborn child is all id and only later does it develop an ego and superego.

The ego, Freud theorized, is "that part of the id which has been modified by the direct influence of the external world." The ego is the arbiter between id's unrealistic, fantasy-oriented unconscious desires and the realities of the external world. Instead of working on the pleasure principle, ego works on what Freud called the *reality principle,* which is aimed at satisfying id's demands in more realistic ways with due consideration to societal norms and rules. However, both the id and the ego have one common thread—seeking pleasure and avoiding pain. If the id is the horse, ego is its rider, according to Freud.

Finally, the superego is embedded in the part of our mind that knows the difference between right and wrong and creates the feeling of guilt when a wrong act is committed. The superego uses morals and values learned from parents and society as its building blocks. It starts developing when an infant reaches the ages of three to five years, a stage of growth referred to as psychosexual development. Similar to the ego, the superego's job is to manage the id's impulses, especially sex and aggression.

Therefore, there's a moral aspect to the superego that has two parts: the conscience and the ideal self. We all know conscience quite well since we have all felt guilt at some point in our lives. We also recognize the ideal self as someone we aspire to be as a human being, parent, spouse, sibling, son, daughter, professional, and solid member of society. It is interesting to note that the image of the ideal self is derived from our observations of the world, parental expectations, and societal norms. Unlike the id, we are not born with an image of the ideal self. It is created over time. When we become the ideal self, the superego rewards us with the feeling of pride, which is uplifting, joyful, and even addictive.

There's an interesting aspect of pride that was revealed in the studies conducted by scientists like Dr. Judson Brewer. In an effort to try to break the vicious cycle of substance abuse, he studied the effect of ego states and addictive states on brain activity. When subjects were asked to focus on themselves, akin to egoistic thinking, and their brain activity was measured, a distinct part of the brain "lit up" or showed above-average activity with neurons firing rapidly. When that happens, there are certain physiological reactions that take place in our body, and chemicals released in the process fill us with pride, a sense of confidence, and joy. Perhaps the most interesting fact in this study is that this is the same part of the brain that shows hyperactivity in subjects addicted to cocaine and other substances. In other words, ego or thinking about self is scientifically shown to activate the same area of the brain that addictive substances light up. One can extrapolate reasonably, therefore, that ego is likely highly addictive and, in its progressive stages, can morph into narcissism and ultimately into hubris.

On the other hand, withdrawal from ego, just like from any addictive substance or chemical, can be extremely painful but cleansing. Meditation camps like Vipassana are "rehab clinics" for the ego. While we all know substance abuse to be extremely harmful and potentially fatal, ego addiction feels good and does not seem to create any physical harm. Little do we realize that it can keep our soul immersed in the darkness of emotional suffering our entire life. Enlightened beings have advised time and again against feeding this ego. But the addiction of the self is extremely hard to break because it has been conditioned over the years as a necessary element of self-preservation and happiness. If the studies by Dr. Brewer are any indication, ego becomes hardwired in our brain and would require complete rewiring of the circuits of our intelligence center.

It may not come as a surprise, therefore, that when some of us achieve the image of the "ideal" self as our caretakers expected, especially after years of efforts to acquire worldly pleasures, comforts, career, power, and prestige, the thick shadow of hubris blinds us and plunges us into the dark recesses of pride. When pride gets out of control and becomes highly addictive and narcissistic, hubris is born. Thus completing the connection between ego and hubris.

This background information, while academic, is important in a layperson's understanding of the concept of ego and hubris.

Almost every organized religion and spiritual belief system preaches the destruction of ego—the "I", "Me," and "Mine"—if we are to receive the blessings of God. It is a central concept even in belief systems, like Buddhism and Jainism, where the concept of God assumes a different definition and meaning. Universally, ego is considered the biggest obstacle in our journey toward nirvana, salvation, enlightenment, or acquiring even the simplest form of peace and happiness. It is the obstacle that causes many to stumble and get hurt, sometimes irreparably, in their journey to build successful relationships, to love, to give compassion, and to discover their own truth. Ego is the darkest shadow that fills the divide that separates us from our Creator. We all know this fact at some level and yet most of us fall victim to the addictive powers of ego.

We are born with a very simple pleasure principle: we want immediate gratification of our desire because that's exactly what we got when we were in our mother's womb. In fact, we did not even have to ask for anything; it was automatically provided. Our mother was looking after us with so much love that she could anticipate our desires instinctively. That was perfect union! We did not even have to express our demands because there was no gap between our desires and the source of their satisfaction, our Creator. We were conditioned in this perfect state of peace and contentment for nine months. It is our separation from our

Creator at birth that initiated the journey from the pleasure principle (the id) to the reality principle (the ego).

When we examine the definitions of the three human dimensions—the id, the ego, and the superego—it is not surprising to find phrases like *hidden desires of the id (the unconscious mind); fantasy oriented; modified by the realities of the external world; and feelings of guilt.* If we consider *hidden desires of the id,* we cannot help but associate it with our craving to merge with the unlimited, our God, our Mother, our Creator.

This hidden desire of our unconscious mind is unpolluted, intense, and innocent during the first three to five years of life. As we grow, however, the concept of ego and superego starts to take shape through the external realities of the world. Somewhere during this period of "growth" the innocence of id is overpowered by the burning desires of our ego while superego becomes our sounding board of morality. And we get caught in the inextricable addiction of pleasure offered by our ego and the sense of morality that superego manifests. It appears to many of us that the answer to lasting happiness lies hidden somewhere between the pride and moral conduct, both of which are fruits of a society created by the very mortal beings that are afflicted by the same disease. Is it any wonder that most of us get lost in our quest to find happiness and eventually resign to live a life that looks like everyone else's? We conform so we can be considered "normal," just like society intended. We want to fit in. We look for acceptance by others as an affirmation that we are okay, that we are loved. As we look to history for answers, all enlightened souls were considered abnormal and were ridiculed, judged, tortured, and even sacrificed simply because they challenged the status quo. It's the same abnormal souls that many of us now look up to with reverence for guidance. If we find our inner Buddha, we can get closer to them. Just a couple of small adjustments and we can live a more normal, fulfilling life while benefiting society even as we become different in many ways that some may consider "abnormal."

The Traditional View: We are conditioned to believe that ego is our friend since it is designed to give us a sense of pride, our raison d'être, and a respectable place in society—necessary ingredients to achieve happiness. We follow the rules of the society and conduct ourselves in the best manner possible, using superego as our litmus test. We keep accumulating the material comforts to stoke our pride, all in our quest to achieve happiness, contentment, tranquility, and lasting peace. However, when we get to the so-called promised land of sensual and material pleasures, we find ourselves just as naked emotionally as we were at birth.

The evidence of this disappointment and the desperation is present in addictions and suicides committed by famous personalities who achieved the zenith of fame and wealth. Despite such stark evidence, politicians, the elite, and even self-anointed saints continue to thrive on ego. Those who surround these figures fortify their belief and accentuate their ego. Using the lens of the traditional view, ego is, therefore, considered to be desirable when it is supported by material success. However, even the so-called supporters who stand by the side of the powerful and the mighty secretly abhor this human state.

Religion, while blind to its own ego, almost universally considers human ego to be an obstacle in our journey toward peace and happiness. It's no surprise that religion and other belief systems universally advise that we keep our ego in check and, if possible, annihilate it completely. Doing so could lead to nirvana or enlightenment, as experienced by some like Gautama Buddha and Guru Nanak. I don't believe enlightenment to be a permanent state of bliss. I believe it is a mental tool to constructively process suffering. It is simply the reshaping of the lens through which we witness and process the material and sensual world. To be sure, all enlightened souls experienced suffering too. But they had attained enlightenment that helped them process suffering in a way that it did not affect their deep sense of peace. Compassion for themselves and for everything external to them was the ingredient used to fashion this tool.

The Wah! Perspective: If we adorn the lens of karunā and look at ego with empathy, what we will discover is that our motivation to achieve the ideal image is driven by our primal and pure desire to find happiness, contentment, and peace. We want to return to the same state of permanent bliss we experienced in our mother's womb. Unfortunately, the tools we are provided and the way we are shown by our caretakers leads us to another destination. They meant well from their heart and soul because they did not know any other way. The lens through which they saw life became colored by the apparent brightness and glitter of the external world, or maya. Little did they realize that this glitter was darkness veiled to fool their unsuspecting eyes. The layers of darkness that filled their Gap prevented them from showing us the true path toward self-fulfillment.

The resulting obscurity in our own Gap frustrates our attempts to find the Light. Sometimes the frustration transforms our pride into anger, anxiety, stress, and even hubris that causes real harm to our relationships and to us. Even this extreme human condition has its source in the pure desire to reach the Creator. In a way, hubris is to an adult what the id is to an infant—the need to satisfy desire without any delay and without regard for the consequences.

However, it's not a hopeless situation. Illusions created by the external realities of the world, when cleansed, bring about the realization that our separation from our Creator was also an illusion—we were never separated. The darkness of ego—our own shadow—simply got in the way of the Light. To quote Mikhail Naimy again, "The shadowless only are in the light. The shadowless only know one God. For God is Light, and Light alone is able to know Light."

There are effective and proven ways to recognize our ego, and then through the practice of loving-kindness and compassion for ourselves, place checks and balances so it doesn't get out of control. Sustained practice of these simple techniques will, over time, cultivate the most potent antidote of ego—humility. It is humility that placed so many souls on the path to enlightenment. While only very few us can hope to become enlightened, many of us can achieve lasting states of bliss and happiness through the practice of humble karunā.

All of us are addicted to something—ego, substances, sensual pleasures, material wealth—because we are all broken in some way and disconnected to our source of true happiness, our Higher Self. We fail to unify our duality—the good and the evil, the kind and the cruel—and hence, happiness eludes us. Until we find a way to unify our opposing parts through our consciousness and balance our souls, the tentacles of anxiety, fear, and depression will keep us entrapped. This trilogy can firmly grip some of us when our repeated attempts to find happiness fail. To escape the trilogy's tentacles some resort to psychotherapy, medications, or alternative methodologies like yoga and meditation, while others find safe harbor in addictive behaviors that become vicious cycles and cause downward spirals with irreparable harm. Most of us, however, can avoid becoming entangled and trapped in the web spun by anxiety, fear, and depression through cultivation and practice of humility and self-compassion.

5

anxiety, fear, and depression

Does the restless surface of the ocean know that it can find peace and tranquility in its own depths?

During the same visit to Costa Rica in April 2009 when the river shifted the direction of my life through a new appreciation of love and life, there was another incident that perfectly highlights how ego can lead to tremendous anxiety and even to ultimate peril. This is not hyperbole but a real account of an incident, the likes of which take place all over the world. Sometimes they are labeled as foolish acts that should never have been undertaken in the first place. It's easy to offer such opinions after the fact. One has to wonder, however, what happens in the heat of the moment that we end up engaging in careless actions that can literally undermine our precious life? The answer in my case was pure ego—my sense of self, of pride, of being in control.

I was part of a group of students who had gathered in Costa Rica to learn and practice the art of surfing, photography, and yoga. To make the program more attractive, the school had organized additional activities. One day we all trekked through a beautiful rainforest to a clearing that opened up to a small, uninhabited beach with nothing but brightly colored kayaks lined up in a row. Ever since early adulthood, I had harbored the fear of deep water, as I had almost drowned during an early morning display of bravado in a swimming pool, even though I barely knew how to swim at the time. Despite my fear and anxiety of entering deep waters, I was swept into groupthink because everyone was excited about kayaking in the ocean. I did not want to be seen as a wimp. I wanted to fit in. So, despite my deep-seated fear of deep water, I agreed to try it.

It was a hot and humid sunny day with a light breeze cooling off our perspiration. We strapped on our bright-red life jackets and off we went—one to each equally colorful kayak. The going was smooth, and I was nervously enjoying the soft lapping of the waves against the kayak. The sound of the oars hitting the water was rather musical. I could hear the excitement in the voice of my co-kayakers who had pulled ahead of me. So far so good, I thought and smiled nervously. Then I crossed a sandbar and the wave pattern shifted. I could see big waves crashing against a massive rock formation around the corner. By now, I had lost sight of everyone, including the guide, as they had already gone around the rock. I tried to stay calm and worked hard to maintain control of the kayak. The force of the ocean was far stronger than I was. I felt my body stiffen and jaw tighten. As my heart started to race, I could feel panic setting in. I tried shouting for help, but the sound of the ocean hitting the rock drowned out my weak cries. I barely had a voice. I looked back at the shore, and it seemed within reach only if I could turn the kayak. But the waves were pushing me farther away. I froze and stopped moving altogether and felt my end was near. Then I saw one yellow kayak come around the bend. It was the guide. He must have taken a count and found one kayaker missing. After some struggle, he was able to thaw me out of my frozen state and gradually guide me to the shore. That day would mark the last time I would enter a kayak or the deep ocean!

As I think about that day, I realize that this story is a metaphor for how our ego often gets the better of us. We expect that things will turn out okay if we are in control. And when circumstances change for the worse, we find ourselves helpless or frozen by fear or anxiety. As we try to control the situation with more force, it only gets worse. In such a state of despair, only our inner "guide" can show us the path to a place where we can feel safe and find peace again. We will get to the topic of this "guide" in the last chapter of the book.

The Cambridge English Dictionary defines anxiety as "an uncomfortable feeling of nervousness or worry about something that is happening or might happen in the future ... something that causes a feeling of fear and worry."

One may conclude from this definition that all dimensions of anxiety are bad. But in fact, anxiety is a very "normal" human emotion that can be good in certain situations. For example, if you stand at the edge of the Niagara Falls or the Grand Canyon and look down, you may feel anxious, nervous, or dizzy. That's your brain sending you warning signals so you can step away from the danger. Heeding those signals is generally a smart idea for self-preservation. This is where anxiety can be a catalyst for normal, self-protective behavior.

However, we normally associate anxiety with abnormal behavioral disorders, and psychologists regularly see patients with some extreme conditions of anxiety, including those who experience panic attacks, uncommon fear even under normal life conditions, and those in whom anxiety leads to depression of varying degrees. Psychologists have shown that anxiety becomes heightened on the anniversary date of traumatic events. Some people are known to have anxiety attacks on their birthdays—perhaps the separation from their Creator is still fresh in some part of their brain. One can only extrapolate this finding to understand the plight of those who repeatedly suffer trauma like sexual, physical, or emotional abuse over a number of years. It's almost impossible for them to find a break in their lives that can be filled with a semblance of peace. Psychologists believe that such trauma biologically lives in every cell of the abused person's body. It becomes part of who they are, literally. It should not come as a surprise, therefore, that those who have witnessed or experienced trauma or abuse suffer from unusual symptoms related to fear and depression very frequently.

Fear, like anxiety, is also a natural survival instinct that we experience under conditions that threaten our normal life. Hence, absolute darkness, the growl of a ferocious animal, a sudden loud sound or foolishly entering the ocean in a kayak evokes one of four responses—freeze, fight, flight, or faint. When that happens a number of physiological responses take place in our body almost instantly. We experience sweaty palms, a rapid heart rate, flaring nostrils to allow more oxygen into the body, a dilation of pupils, and even a relaxation of the muscles around the anus. By personal experience I can tell you that they can all happen at the same time! Adrenaline kicks in within nanoseconds, as our body prepares us for one of the four responses.

The understanding that The Gap provides to explain anxiety, fear, and depression is simple and natural. Psychologists agree that trauma can create anxiety, and they also agree that the more severe the trauma, the more pronounced the anxiety associated with it. Imagine then what the most traumatic experience of our life—our birth—did to hardwire our brain with anxiety. The trauma at birth was literally captured and stored in every cell of our body. Is it any surprise then that psychologists consider anxiety to be a "normal" part of every human being's set of natural emotions? New scientific evidence points to the possibility of a baby experiencing anxiety while inside the womb, especially if the mother undergoes stressful life circumstances. Extreme stress suffered by a mother can induce premature birth or separation from the Creator. The baby can likely feel it and, therefore, exhibits this fear and anxiety even in the womb.

Separation anxiety experienced at birth is indelibly impressed in our consciousness, and it continues to plague us in every situation where the least bit of uncertainty pervades. It never goes away. It simply lies dormant when life is running smoothly and according to plan because we feel a sense of control, as false and temporary as it may be. One nudge of uncertainty or a feeling that we are losing control, just like we did at birth, and the pangs of anxiety wake up from dormant sleep.

The metaphor of the kayak exemplifies how turbulent events in our life bring bouts of anxiety that are so severe at times that they cause panic, stress, and, at times, utter chaos and desperate attempts to find normalcy. Fear, the immediate offshoot of anxiety, can then consume our psyche. If we begin to feel hopeless that the circumstances cannot be changed in our favor, anxiety and fear grow deeper roots that nourish panic, depression, and even suicidal thoughts. But there's hope. If nature gave us anxiety at birth, it also blessed us with an incredible antidote that's far more powerful and always available without even trying—our breath!

A simple and conscious awareness at all times that our Creator, our soul, our Higher Self always lives in our own depths can bring us peace and calm, even though He may be separated from our limited awareness and physical form. There's no better way to remind us of our Inner Self than with the process of breathing because it does not require us to exert any effort—it happens instinctively and naturally, just like in the womb. A few deep inhalations through the nose and slow exhalations through the mouth have the capacity to instill some restfulness in us because our breath reminds us that we are alive and that we are present. Our breath has a mystical power to connect us with our Inner Self, albeit temporarily. Those who practice mindfulness meditation by concentrating on their breath report experiencing a sense of calm that's surreal, durable, and mystical.

Pranayama, a breathing technique practiced by yogis, literally means regulating the breath (prāna, a Sanskrit word, means breath, and yama means regulation). The virtues of prānayama have been recognized for thousands of years in Ayurveda, the ancient science of health and living. Simple breathing exercises have the power to release beneficial chemicals in our body, a fact that even modern medicine now recognizes. These chemicals act as an antidote to anxiety, slow down our heart rate, and soothe our mind by sending enough oxygen to every cell in our body. The idea that something as complex as anxiety weaving intricate, troubling scenarios in our mind can be effectively calmed by something as simple as pranayama or meditation is not easily believable. But studies show otherwise. Even if you don't suffer from anxiety, try some deep breathing to calm your mind. Some wise meditators say, "The mind goes where the breath is" and vice versa. The calmer the breath, the calmer the mind. There's a Sanskrit saying about the linkage of mind and the attitude toward life, "Manā eva manusyanām karanām bandhā moksāyoh," which means, "As the mind, so the person; bondage or liberation is in your own mind." I experience this effect most mornings and evenings during my twenty-minute meditations. The breath almost comes to a halt when the mind is calm. Perhaps it's the breath that's calming the mind. Regardless, the result is a serene feeling that's unmatched.

Patanjali, in *The Yoga Sutras of Patanjali* (aphorisms), one of the most celebrated works on yoga, health, and longevity, lays out the benefits of deep breathing. According to Patanjali, deep breathing has the ability to remove our "identity" (ego) and other obstacles on the path toward attainment of peace and fulfillment. This happens simply because what's already present inside us reveals itself fully over time through mindful breathing. Meditative practices produce similar miraculous effects on many. A legendary Hollywood director of many hit movies admitted to managing his anxiety and panic attacks through Transcendental Meditation, or TM, another meditative technique designed to soothe the mind and slow down the breathing. Many other popular figures in contemporary history have provided accounts of how meditation and yoga breathed a new life into their souls, cured addictions, and brought longer and more durable peace. Famous personalities such as Katy Perry, Oprah Winfrey, Jerry Seinfeld, Howard Stern, Ellen DeGeneres, and Arianna Huffington practice meditation because they believe in its physical and emotional benefits.

Research conducted at prestigious universities like Harvard and Stanford continues to show persistent evidence that deep breathing, meditation, and simple mindfulness exercises can have long-lasting beneficial effects on our health and can even cure addictions. Dr. Sara Lazar, a Harvard Medical School instructor in psychology, found that just eight weeks of mindfulness meditation, which anchors on breathing, appears to produce measurable changes in the regions of the brain that are associated with not only our sense of self, but also those connected to memory, empathy, and stress. In fact, the study showed that those who practiced an average of twenty-seven minutes of daily mindfulness meditation showed an increased density of gray matter in regions of the brain associated with introspection, compassion, and self-awareness. Additionally, those who experienced a reduction in stress showed a lower density of gray matter in the amygdala, the region of the brain associated with anxiety and stress. So, our breath may hold the secret to managing anxiety, fear, and depression without subjecting ourselves to long sessions on the proverbial psychoanalyst's couch or to chemicals with the goal of removing the darkness, so our inner Light can begin to reveal itself.

The Traditional View: We generally regard anxiety and depression as mental disorders that need medical attention, especially if they become debilitating. Medical intervention is indeed necessary for such patients. The question I keep asking myself is why do we experience such incapacitating ailments related to our brain? In some ways, these are more dangerous than ailments that one can observe physically. Anxiety and depression are silent predators that invade our minds and wreak havoc in our lives.

One reason could be that our society seems to have lost some of its simplicity and innocence. The expectations to succeed, accumulate material comforts, pursue sought-after careers, and build wealth for a secure future have become part of our fabric. We expect instant gratification—the kind Freud described when explaining the id in young children. For example, teenagers, youth, and adults alike get sucked into social media that further perpetuate the id syndrome. If we don't receive a reply to our text within nanoseconds, we watch the phone's screen for signs that the receiver of the text is typing a response. We check the time when the text was delivered, and anxiety takes hold if we don't see a response within a New York minute. One doesn't need scientific studies to notice the heightened stress level and anxiety among teenagers and others who are addicted to social media and smartphones. One of my very good friends, a CEO of a multinational company, routinely checks his e-mail every time he wakes up in the middle of the night. It is not unusual to receive his response at 3:00 a.m. Sleep is nature's way of de-stressing our brain and giving rest to our body. I wonder what such a habit is doing to his mental and physical health.

Another reason why we seem to be under the constant effect of stressors could be the perceived or explicit expectations of others. Parents and caretakers want the best for their children and pass along the same advice they received when they were young. We end up buying into their "truth" and make it our own. Even when we achieve what was expected of us, true peace and happiness still eludes us. As a result, seeds of anxiety and depression begin to sprout. Curious clouds of hopelessness and emptiness cast long shadows, and our inner Light starts to dim.

There are many other triggers of anxiety—disease, romantic breakups, divorce, death, loss of a home, hereditary mental disorders, moving because of a job, termination from a job—and the list goes on and on without an end in sight. It is possible that for every anxious or depressed person there's a different reason and a trigger that pushes that individual into the cesspool of anxiety and depression.

It's not surprising, therefore, that psychotherapists and psychiatrists are busier than ever and rehab facilities are filled with young and old alike. The National Institutes of Health reports that in 2014 approximately 43.6 million or 18.1 percent of US adults suffered from some form of mental illness. The news gets even worse. The Centers for Disease Control and Prevention (CDC) finds: "Antidepressants were the third most common prescription drug taken by Americans of all ages in 2005-2008 and the most frequently used by persons aged 18-44 years. From 1988-1994 through 2005-2008, the rate of antidepressant use in the United States among all ages increased nearly 400%." These are very disturbing trends. Depression and anxiety, therefore, are more common than we believe because they are silent diseases. They exist in the deep recesses of a person's brain.

If someone we love suffers from anxiety or panic disorder, our concern is valid because, if unaddressed, the consequences can be severe. We generally view these states negatively and blame both nature and nurture for their presence.

The Wah! Perspective: As mentioned earlier, it is logical and likely that separation anxiety begins at birth and that it is related to the separation from our Creator, our Inner Self. The seed of anxiety, fear, and depression is planted in us at that time. If we view the states of anxiety and depression through the lens of karunā, we find that separation from our Higher Self is the common factor underlying all such human conditions. Whether it is losing a loved one or feeling trapped in a kayak in the middle of the ocean, almost all states of anxiety occur because we fear being separated from our Creator before we have had a chance to meet Him. Some fear separation from loved ones; some from the worldly and sensual pleasures; and some others from an awesome career path—the objects are countless, but the underlying reason is the same...separation from our perceived sense of happiness. Even in death we fear the same. Because we are human.

We all know from the physics experiments in high school that white light, when passed through a prism, breaks up into its component colors of a beautiful rainbow. We see the same effect when sunlight passes through a layer of misty rain and, magically, a rainbow appears in the distance. What's also true is that if you cover the prism with a plastic film of red color and then shine the white light through it, the resulting rainbow will be missing the red hue. Similarly, when the Light of the Creator passes through the prism of our soul, any dirt or "coloring" built up by belief systems and the environment in which we are nurtured will not allow the life's rainbow to emerge with the glory of all its colors. Some colors will be suppressed. There will be nothing but emptiness in place of those colors. If these colors happen to be those of self-confidence and self-awareness, anxiety will likely fill that gap.

Karunā helps us understand this state of emptiness and its true cause. Just like a restless child is calmed by the soothing and compassionate caress of her mother, karunā, or loving-kindness, has the power to push the seeds of anxiety, fear, and depression into a state of dormancy. People afflicted with this "mental disorder" simply need compassionate understanding and a loving dialogue. Addictions, suicidal thoughts, and severe panic attacks can be effectively addressed though karunā. Medicine and therapy are supplements, but a genuine desire to remove someone's pain is the foundation for bringing peace and tranquility to the restless lives of many. The life's rainbow can be restored to all its glory through simple acts of loving-kindness. If you know someone who suffers from anxiety, panic attacks, or depression, try giving them a compassionate hug, a patient ear, and words of loving-kindness. You will be surprised at the results.

It will not only bring a calmer disposition to the one who is afflicted by this terrible, invisible disease, but you will also experience a strange sense of peace and tranquility. Brain waves are infectious!

We must, however, recognize that some of our anxiety stems from our belief systems that are learned behaviors or impressions since our birth. At the purest level, our soul is not anxious or fearful or depressed. It is eternally joyful. Closely associated with anxiety are belief systems that make us feel guilty and even "dirty." Some of these beliefs we call sins. Whether promulgated by organized religion or taught to us by our caretakers, sin is a very real concept that afflicts an inordinately large number of people. In fact, anyone who is religious has felt the pang of sin at some point in time. Confession of sin is a common way to purge oneself of anxiety created by this guilt. And yet, the guilt never goes away, as the sin returns with all its fury. In many cultures, there's a close connection of sin with sex and sexuality. It's a very real issue that only a few face or can face head on due to a variety of reasons that are far too complex to delve into at this time. So, we will stick to examining the relationship between sex and sin.

6

sex and Sin

"The first and greatest punishment of the sinner is the conscience of sin."

— *Lucius Annaeus Seneca*

At a very personal level, I believed for over two decades that my father's suicide was God's way of punishing me for my sin. I had planned a one-week vacation to celebrate my twenty-third birthday with a beautiful and charming Indian-American woman. She was going to make a special trip from the United States to Bangalore, India, where I worked and lived. I had reserved a corporate bungalow in the peaceful hills of Ooty, a serene place for lovers just north of Bangalore. Such escapes between unmarried couples were extremely rare in India's conservative society and definitely not blessed by parents, as they were considered immoral and sinful. I felt privileged and excited for what awaited me despite my internal struggle. The hormones were firing from every cell and were winning the war. The imagined passion was far stronger than any thought of sinful action. Romantic scenarios laced with sensual ones dominated my thoughts. She was to arrive in Bangalore on January 1, 1988. However, on December 31, 1987, at 7:30 a.m., everything changed. I was woken up by loud knocks on my apartment door. It was my landlord. He said my brother was on the phone and he sounded urgent. My heart started to race because my brother never called me—long-distance phone calls were expensive and we couldn't afford them. Half asleep and panicked, I rushed down the winding concrete stairway and picked up the receiver. I could barely say hello when my brother spoke in a grave and breaking voice. "Dad has had a serious stroke. He is in the ICU. Come home." I returned home the same afternoon, and the birthday celebration with my Indian-American "girlfriend" never became reality.

While my father lay severely ill, I offered daily prayers at the temple located in the hospital lobby. I asked for God's forgiveness for the sin I was going to commit by having premarital sexual relations. My father got better, and he came home to recuperate. Then he suffered a second stroke. He never recovered from it emotionally. On a hot summer morning on May 28, 1988, he decided to take matters into his own hands and free himself from his agony. I tried to give him CPR, but the rope had done its work. I could not revive him. He was gone. Life had been strangled away from him. God had punished me for my sin. Religious teachings had convinced me, as many other religions have taught other people, that our karmā created the conditions of our human existence. If I followed the "good behavior" preached in temples, churches, mosques, and gurudwaras, I would be able to alleviate my suffering. But if I "sinned," I would have to suffer here and in my future lives. "You reap what you sow" is the closest adage that described the belief system that was embedded in me. So, suffering became the direct result of my actions or "sins." I believed that I had committed a grave sin by not only intending to act on my sexual fantasy but also by engaging in pre-marital sexual behavior. That was enough to provoke God's fury and He had decided to end my father's life as my punishment. I was, therefore, responsible for his death. This was my strong belief for over two decades. My plan to act on it was enough. That was the only thought that echoed in my head for many years after his passing. It still does, although I am better equipped to process it now. This is despite rational and compassionate support from family, friends, and therapists.

My story is not unusual—only the circumstances and the belief systems are different, but we all have similar narratives in our minds that are associated with sin and the emotional toll it takes on our psyche. Sin is a troubling concept that's deeply entrenched in almost every society and in every religion. It is so deeply entangled in our being that it can take a lifetime to shift our way of thinking and our beliefs, if ever.

Some religions banish their otherwise faithful followers to a life in hell for even casting a gaze toward an unmarried woman. Others define sin in a variety of different ways. Every organized religion, for the most part, has a definition of sin that it believes fits its own unique interpretation. It is rigid, it is definite, and it is nonnegotiable. It is generally also contradictory. Apparently, this definition comes directly from God, who, in the same religion is ever-loving and ever-forgiving. He never punishes. How can a god that only knows how to love and forgive also be discriminatory and pass judgment on some actions and make them punishable in the most severe ways? If we are the embodiment of God and His spirit lives in us, as some religions contend, and we commit a sin, isn't God engaging in it too? In fact, isn't it the Supreme Power that commits the sin, but through us? Or is sin a convenient interpretation by the religious guard to protect its own turf by instilling fear and by keeping the reins of forgiveness confined to confessional chambers and ceremonies?

Even at a more academic level, the definition of sin has a strong religious influence. Dictionary.com defines sin as "a transgression of divine law; any act regarded as such a transgression, especially a willful or deliberate violation of some religious or moral principle; any reprehensible or regrettable action, behavior, lapse, etc; great fault or offense."

As this definition suggests and as our experience confirms, the words divine and religion are closely related to sin. Most commonly, much of sin is related to sex or, to be more precise, to sexual conduct. Some religions allow forgiveness simply by confession, and others ask the sinner to undergo difficult penance. Sin is generally born at the junction where right actions end and wrong ones begin. As Freud theorized, we all have a superego that acts as a sounding board between right and wrong. This superego develops after we reach three to five years of age. In other words, it's a nurture effect and not one created by nature. And religion has a big role to play in the development and coloring of our superego. That explains my personal belief system, prayers, and eventual guilt associated with my contemplated "reprehensible action" and "lapse of judgment."

Under society's moral code, sin and sex have an intimate relationship in most religions. My religion is no exception. Sex, on the other hand, also has an intimate relationship with something else that's on the other side of the spectrum of disdainful sin—the pure feeling of love. In fact, some may also consider it a divine act, as it can produce new life. Most of us often feel that sex either lifts us in love or pushes us down with sin when we engage in it simply for sensual pleasure. What about the situation where a couple engages in sex first and then falls in love? Was their sexual conduct sinful? And how about the couple that becomes sexually intimate, falls out of love, and continues to engage in sex? Is their sexual conduct now sinful but was divine while they were in love? Just because they stay married, does the social bond make their sexual conduct pure and not sinful, even when sex becomes a form of physical abuse? Indeed, several married women have reported being "raped" by their husband. The answers are just as confusingly varied depending on who is on the other side of the argument.

Sex, people say, is an essential part of love. How sex is practiced varies based on cultural and social norms. I find it curious that couples in love still refer to sex as "making love." Did they not "make love" as they created and expressed the feelings that love evokes when they fell in love? Or does it imply that they need to continue to make love so they can stay in love? Or does this definition of "making love" mean "making a new life" since a baby is an expression of love between two people? Can we equate love with sex or vice versa? After all, sex is enjoyed by many without a reference or feeling of love imbued in it. The sex trade is, in fact, considered the oldest profession. Clearly, prostitutes don't trade love. They simply offer sensory pleasure, fleeting and temporary as it may be.

Perhaps it's the dual nature of sex—powerful but transient—that acts as a magnet for all animals alike. Sex has this unmatched power over almost all human beings. Nothing else in the palate of human emotions even comes close. Even the deepest emotional needs mellow with time, but the desire for sex remains raw, for a very long time. Anthropologists believe it is the desire to procreate that's hardwired in our brains, which arouses sexual desires in humans. We engage in sexual activity for the sake of the human race's survival. Arguably, self-preservation is a noble cause. Some have, however, used it to justify their hideous actions, even when their partner was either not willing or unable to provide consent. Perhaps nothing has stirred more trouble since time immemorial than sex and its pursuit, legitimate or not.

When sex occurs within the bounds of the religion's moral code, it is not only sanctioned, it is at times considered the purest form of love. Some religions, including some forms of Judaism and Tantric Buddhism, accord sex one of the highest places in life because they consider it a union with the divine. Some native people consider the woman's uterus the center of the Universe's spiritual power because of its role in giving birth to new life. Love is not mentioned in those belief systems around sex—it is implied.

However, once the sanctity of love is broken, and sex becomes an end in itself purely for sensory pleasure, it is sure to lead to undesirable consequences. Addiction, infidelity, sexual abuse, sexual trafficking and the like lurk in such darkness. With precedence and evidence all around us, the offender is "powerless" in the face of insatiable sexual desire. Even presidents and pallbearers of social justice, those living ethically, and those with high moral values have fallen victim to the power of sex. Recent hacking of Ashley Madison's *"Life is short. Have an affair."* website displays how deep the tentacles of sex run into human society. Some are more successful at hiding these activities than others. Those who are exposed, risk losing face in the court of public opinion and oftentimes in the court of their own conscience. Such is the dominance of sex on our psyche—both for those who judge and for those who are judged.

The other dark side of sex is the abuse related to it. A comfortable home, if steeped in darkness, can be a scary place to live and can cause injuries as we stumble over what is otherwise familiar in light; a soul immersed in darkness can also be the cause of angst, fear, and desperate acts.

Sexual abuse is sometimes reported as physical abuse for obvious reasons associated with a true disclosure. Battered women and children, for example, are often sexually abused also. Physical abuse statistics, therefore, can and often include sexual abuse. Before we examine the reasons why abuse occurs let's consider some startling statistics quoted in the National Register of Health Service Psychologists by Dr. Linda Berg-Cross, a clinical psychologist in Potomac, Maryland. In her article titled "Intimate Relationships, Psychological Abuse and Mental Health Problems," she states, *"Almost all women who are physically abused are also verbally abused (84%) and psychologically abused (Follingstad et. al., 1990). • Seventy-two percent of battered women report that emotional abuse had a more severe impact on them than physical abuse (Follingstad et. al., 1990) • Among a group of battered women, 46% of women state that emotional ridicule is the worst type of abuse to experience (Follingstad et. al., 1990) • There is no difference among the races or various ethnic groups on the incidence of physical abuse (Lockhart, 1985; Campbell, 1989) • No research, to date, has systematically examined cultural differences in the prevalence of psychological abuse • Psychological abuse is a significant predictor of depressive symptomatology and problem drinking (Arias, Street, & Brody, 1996) • Psychological abuse is a meaningful predictor of parents who will neglect or maltreat their children (Arias, Street, & Brody, 1996)"* Further, *"both Follingstad et. al. (1990) and Stets (1990) reported that an astounding 99% of battered women experience psychological abuse of some type."*

That's a lot of suffering. Just reading these statistics makes us feel the pain, especially if we have experienced or witnessed such abuse firsthand. The one distinguishing aspect of abuse is that the emotional state of the perpetrator of abuse creates an impact on the abused that, in turn, creates a chain of emotional reactions and devastating results that can last a lifetime and become self-perpetuating in a vicious cycle. In my work with vulnerable and at-risk children in Central America, these sad and alarming statistics become very real. I have also witnessed firsthand how the devastating effects of sexual abuse and its raw reality continues to live in the faces of the innocent children who have to be removed from their families. What's truly disturbing is that many of these children thought the abuse, specifically sexual molestation, was a form of love and, therefore, they cannot understand why they have been removed from their families. Their suffering is multiplied later by the eventual realization of the nature of their experience when extreme feelings of shame and guilt take over. This is not unusual as I have also experienced these emotions first hand.

Strangely, my feelings of shame stemmed from the realization that I may have enjoyed the abuse. Only later did I understand through therapy that there's a difference between physiology and psychology. Nerve endings, when stimulated, created those pleasurable sensations, but what was happening to my consciousness and my psychological makeup was disastrous. It is a known fact that sometimes women experience orgasms even during rape. Clearly, the pain associated with such an orgasm is felt deeply by their soul, and the scar created by this gruesome injury never goes away. At times, such scars are visible in our lives through the paucity of familial and other loving relationships. We forget how to trust anyone or always have our guard raised, even when it feels completely safe. Such a sexual act has nothing whatsoever to do with divinity. It is absolute darkness.

There is no way anyone can justify that it is our desire to merge with the Creator through sex that leads some to abuse others. There's no rational explanation that can support this theory. In fact, it's a shameful and cowardly argument. Then how does one explain this tragic human condition of obsession with sex and its association with sin? Once again, we may have to look through the lens laced with the concept of *The Gap.* A close examination of the root causes of abuse—sexual, physical, or emotional—reveals that a variety of sociopsychological factors are involved. At times, the manifestation of these factors, unfortunately, takes the shape of abuse. What's even more disturbing is that the abused are the weak, the helpless, and the defenseless, at least in the eyes of the abuser. So, rather than simply and squarely placing the blame on the abuser, it might help if we consider an important root cause of abuse. Studies conducted across the globe in different social structures and countries indicate that about one-third of people who are abused in childhood will become abusers themselves. The number is likely higher because many abusers may not remember or may choose not to disclose their own abuse for a variety of reasons. This vicious cycle is one of the worst forms of catch-22 because of the toll it takes on the human psyche. What came first—the abuse or the abuser? Neither can be condoned, but this social issue has deeper roots than what meets the eye.

An article titled *Sad Legacy of Abuse: The Search for Remedies was* authored by Daniel Goleman and published in the *New York Times* in January 1989. It highlights another deeply disturbing social construct: " … a report by William Altemeier, a pediatrician at Vanderbilt University Medical School, and his colleagues, was published in 1986. The strongest predictor from childhood of becoming an abusive parent was not having been abused, but rather having felt as a child that one was unloved and unwanted by one's parents. An attitude common, of course, among abused children, but also found in families in which there is no overt abuse … "

It's worth repeating the strongest predictor of becoming an abusive parent (emphasis added): "*...having felt as a child that one was unloved and unwanted by one's parents...*" As a child, our parents are the embodiment of our Creator. A root cause of abuse, it turns out, is the despair we experience because we feel unloved and unwanted by our Creator. The darkness disconnecting us from the Creator is so overwhelming that it leads some to commit the unthinkable act of hurting the helpless, the weak, and even the loved ones. Acting on these hurtful, predatory instincts adds more darkness to *The Gap* and pushes both the abuser and the abused into a cesspool of complex emotional states.

The hopeful news is that we can at least see and recognize this darkness. The fact that we can see the darkness implies that there's Light behind it. Otherwise, how could anyone witness darkness in the midst of more darkness? We can only see the dark against the light. The solar and the lunar eclipse are visible only because the object that appears dark is blocking the light behind it. It's the light that illuminates the darkness, even when the latter overwhelms it. The reason we can see the stars is because they shine brightly in the dark sky. In fact, the most breathtaking starry nights are observed in the absence of light around us—in pitch darkness on the mountains, in the villages, and in remote areas where there's no light. The most spectacular photographs of the earth taken by satellites are of our blue planet sparkling against the dark abyss. Whether the source of the light is borrowed, as in the case of Earth, or original, as in the case of the sun, darkness must be present to reveal the light. Otherwise, such a phenomenon wouldn't be possible.

The darkness of sexual abuse has other causes. Some would argue that sensual pleasure is perhaps the most powerful aphrodisiac, second only to power—contradicting the respected and wise Henry Kissinger who famously called power "the ultimate aphrodisiac." For some, this powerful aphrodisiac overwhelms all control mechanisms when it becomes addictive. Those afflicted by this disease become completely powerless against the mighty sexual urge—not unlike those addicted to drugs and alcohol—and often require intervention and treatment. Psychologists believe, however, that sexual addiction is often catalyzed by something other than the simple human desire for sexual gratification. It could be deeply buried trauma of sexual abuse, extreme lack of self-confidence, repeated romantic rejections, domestic violence, bullying, or even separation anxiety, in which our neural pathways are affected. The pleasure chemicals released by sexual activity and the simple act of engaging in sex provides a "safe harbor" to those whom we call sex addicts. It provides validation and relevance to the sense of self. Infidelity has a similar foundation, psychologists contend. It has little or nothing to do with the other partner; rather, it has everything to do with the internal dialogue and conflict being experienced by the one committing the unfaithful act. I wonder if it is really a conflict or a deep longing to find something elusive?

Leaving the question of morality and guilt aside for a moment, sexual union with another human being makes both partners feel more relevant and normal *during* the act. This is not to condone the act of infidelity but to explain its construct through an objective psychological lens. It is important to note that the issue of infidelity and its moral judgment is one that's processed by our superego, which, in turn, is created by societal factors. So, what's moral and what's not is a belief system created and judged by society. This layer is intimately woven into the fabric of sin and guilt.

If we look through the mighty power of sex that nature gave to all forms of life, we can see its true virtues and vices. Humans have the intelligence, if they try hard, to lay bare the reasons why sex has so much power over us. All it takes is a simple recall of a memorable, passionate sexual encounter and your body responds physiologically and prepares you to relive it again and again—even in solitude! Every step of the animal dance to seduce a partner—from foreplay to climax—is etched in our brains. If we can recall what makes sex powerful, then a simple deconstruction of this formidable force can help us render it powerless or, at least, reduce its indomitable and, at times, immoral or sinful hold on us. This does not mean that we have to give up sex or stop enjoying the pleasures of the body. Such awareness simply allows us to understand the transient nature of these pleasures to prevent their permanent grasp on our mental framework. It allows us to better control the uncontrollable urges.

We accept morality as a code for good living. Interestingly, however, sex, whether moral or immoral, leaves many self-aware mortals feeling the same way—with a short span of pleasure followed by emptiness. The difference is one of degree and depth by which the darkness of guilt, sin, or emptiness fills The Gap. Since the sensory effects of sex are so powerful, despite their very short life, we confuse them with the sought-after lasting pleasure and fulfillment we seek. Even with an awareness and understanding of its transient nature, we return to it with enthusiasm time and time again, regardless of whether it's powered by the force of love, lust, infidelity, or addiction. Unfortunately, this power sometimes shows its ugly head in rape, incest, abuse, and other forms of nonconsensual sex.

Why does transient sensual pleasure wield so much power over us? When we are engaged in the act of consensual sex, our mind is completely devoid of any other thought except the journey of the sensual experience and the pleasure associated with it. Nothing else in that moment matters. It's almost meditative. In fact, it is just like meditation with only one major difference. While meditation is generally associated with a restful posture and a peaceful mind, sex is filled with movement, physical activity, and immense turmoil in the mind. Both have the same end goal—pleasure and joy. Science proves sex's hold on us through the analysis of hormones and neurotransmitters released in our bloodstream—oxytocin, serotonin, dopamine—which are associated with feelings of pleasure, peacefulness, and overwhelming feelings of love.

When it is over, most people go through a familiar cycle of feelings that goes something like this, in this order: feeling of love, pleasure, relief, satisfaction, indifference, exhaustion, and sleep. Soon after the act, most partners turn away from each other, excuse themselves to use the bathroom, grab a drink, go out on the balcony for a smoke—anything to get us away from the one we just made love to. This behavior is more prevalent among many men. Some feel emptiness soon thereafter and want their partner out of sight. Some ask the question, "Is this it?" Yet others, who have become more self-aware and introspective over time, begin to recognize the transient nature of this powerful intoxicant. Science shows that even our own hormones become less "faithful" and leave our side and our bloodstream soon after the act is over.

While some stay trapped in its vicious cycle, others become seekers and use this understanding as a springboard for spiritual awakening. Seekers realize that the joy and satisfaction—perhaps even contentment—that sex offers is fleeting at best. Lasting peace continues to remain elusive. Ironically, it is the pain of emptiness after the pleasurable but transient sex that can act as a catalyst for the seeker to begin a journey of transformation toward lasting peace and fulfillment. Those who believe sex is divine receive the affirmation of their belief in such transformation. At a minimum, sex's aphrodisiacal power has the potential to become a potent ingredient in the recipe of human transformation.

Maybe it's that fleeting glimpse of the sublime Light during sexual union that brings us back to it time and time again. Perhaps that's why those who are abused or have suffered trauma seek the shelter in sex addiction because they find solace in a repeated, albeit brief and temporary, vision of a place where life can be peaceful and joyful. Perhaps it is this unbridled pursuit of sensory pleasures that promises a view of the Divine that leads some into the world of infidelity. For them, the focus on the limited body makes it impossible to reach the unlimited soul. For others, the feelings associated with sex and all forms of sensual pleasures are so powerful that they can sense the power of something mysterious. Sensuality connects them with something deep, something strong, something they crave and something they love. Perhaps their subconscious finds a hint of their Higher Self in it.

Maybe sexual acts are a vain attempt to close *The Gap* between the Creator and our mortal awareness. Indeed, the repeated emptiness caused by the fruitless pursuit of sensual pleasures can have a miraculous affect on some. It can create an awareness and an understanding that the craving for sensual gratification is a source of suffering—that this suffering can end if we recognize the powerless nature of sex in helping us unite with our Creator for more than just a brief moment.

Sex, in the darkness of silence, creates the magic of life; sex, in the darkness of silence, can also cause much turmoil and suffering in life; and sex, through its irresistible power, also has the ability to put some on the path to ending the darkness in life. It is through this understanding of the yin and the yang, the good and the bad, the power and the powerlessness, the darkness and the light, the love and the despair of sensual pleasures that we can hope to find the tranquility and the contradictions in our own depths. Such awareness can trigger the start of a new journey toward fulfillment.

Many naturally begin this journey during what some call the "midlife crisis" and I call "midlife awakening." When we get to middle age and begin the process of introspection, we recognize the futility in this passion but pursue it nonetheless, albeit with lesser frequency. For some, self-actualization takes the form of reflecting on and resolving the past that is filled with feelings of both guilt and pleasure. Ironically, pleasures keep us captive while guilt, shame and other "negative" narratives can act as a catalyst for life's liberating journey—freedom from the shackles of transient sensual and material pleasures. As humans, it's hard to break the shackles of pleasure. Hence, only very few are able to break lose and move toward the Light.

My favorite poet, Rabindranath Tagore, describes the tumultuous state of mind of the person who is at the precipice of such a transformation—ready to fly but imprisoned by deeply entrenched material and sensual attachments:

Obstinate are thy shackles, and my heart aches when I try to break them.

Freedom is all I want; but to hope for it, I feel ashamed.

I am certain that priceless wealth is in You and that You are my best friend,

But I have not the heart to sweep away the tinsel that fills my room.

The shroud that covers me is a shroud of dust and death; I hate it, yet hug it in love.

My debts are large, my failures great, my shame secret and heavy; yet when I come to ask for my good, I quake in fear lest my prayer be granted.

The Traditional View: Society's view of sin is informed mostly by religious doctrines and the definitions of morality. Most religions believe that sin is related to our actions or karmā and can affect our psyche in good and bad ways. Sin is also most commonly associated with sex, although there are other moral constructs that are considered sinful. While some religions permit confessions of sin and allow for forgiveness, others punish acts that are considered immoral or sinful. Sometimes such punishments are meted out in public so others can "learn a lesson" and not commit the same mistake. It is not uncommon for the media to carry news about public floggings, stonings, and even beheadings in some radical cultures and religions. Sin, for most religious cultures, is the path to hell while moral behavior can assure our passage to heaven. Clearly, the definitions of hell and heaven are designed to elicit the appropriate reactions from those who believe in such norms.

The big elephant in the room for the large majority of believers in heaven and hell, however, is this simple question: why does anyone commit any sin, especially if we believe that the consequence will not be pleasant? It's difficult to answer this question when we consider that humans are, arguably, rational animals. We need the lens of karunā to solve this puzzle.

The Wah! Perspective: Sin, in all its nakedness, is any act that negatively impacts the purity of our soul and disturbs its tranquility. Such disturbance causes the mud of guilt and shame to rise and cloud the view to our pure soul. We lose sight of our own authenticity. And if our inauthentic actions end up changing the course of life of another human being, it's perhaps the gravest of sins. Pure evil is the extreme form of such sin.

However, all the above definitions of sin are generally informed by religion or society. In absence of the conditioning that creates our superego, would we know whether our actions are sinful or not? In fact, would there be such a thing as "sin?" These questions do not challenge or invalidate the premise that society needs a moral compass, an order and a code of conduct so that fellow human beings can coexist peacefully and with love. Perhaps the more important question to ask is whether such a society is possible without the guilt and shame and all the negative aspects related to sin. Had it not been for society's interpretation, would a sinful act ever be born? I don't have the answer. Mikhail Naimy, in *The Book of Mirdad,* does give us one. He writes: "There is no sin in God, unless it be a sin for the Sun to give of his light to a candle. Nor is there sin in Man, unless it be sin for a candle to burn itself away in the Sun and thus be joined unto the Sun."

However, if we view sin through a compassionate lens, we feel empathy for the person whose actions are in question. Why would anyone in their rational mind commit an act that resigns them to a fate of ridicule, public rebuke, and internal struggle filled with shame and guilt? Why would anyone willfully commit acts against their own authentic nature? There must be a force much stronger than the simple desire for sensual pleasure that pushes some past the moral boundaries.

With karunā, we can understand that such a force is the hardwired desire to seek happiness, even though some desperate acts are considered sinful by society. While we cannot dismiss the terrible pain some acts can inflict on others, the question is one of motivation. What drives people to commit such acts? As heinous, harmful, and misguided as these actions are, the raw force behind them is the pure and authentic desire to find peace and happiness, to feel relevant, accepted, and loved. The gift of forgiveness allows us to see through the veil of sin. The sinner, at his or her core, also has the same soul as the rest of us. The only difference is that *The Gap* of the sinner is filled with deep darkness, even as the consciousness continuously searches for the Light. The sinner is addicted to these acts because even temporary relief from anxiety and pain gives hope to the subconscious that lasting peace may be around the corner. Hence, the sinner stays trapped in the shackles of sinful pleasures.

Even those who do not commit sexual sin but engage in sex out of love and moral conduct become prisoners of their desires. Most, if not all, want to capture this feeling forever and through any means. Society gives them permission to do so through marriage.

7

love, marriage, and divorce

Love is the beautiful ornament that is born from two hearts of gold going through life's fires.

When I visited a palmist in India, he reassured my father that all his financial and health ills would soon be a distant memory. How did he know? Curiosity got the better of me, and I asked him to read my palm also. His clairvoyant spirit told him that my father will become rich beyond his imagination and that he will live a healthy life till age eighty-seven. He couldn't have been more wrong. We never recovered from the precipice of financial peril during my father's life, and my father died at fifty-seven. I only remember one aspect of his prediction related to my life—that I would have a tough love life because he had never seen such a "break" in anyone's heart line. Clearly, I thought, he couldn't be right about it because of how wrong he was about my father's future. But he was. He nailed it! I was perhaps the unluckiest person in "capturing" romantic love. All my romantic interludes in high school and college came crashing down in all their glory. But it appears that my "heart line" has finally mended itself. Maybe it's just self-love.

Love, of the numerous human conditions, is considered by many to be immensely powerful, pure, and almost divine, even when the union between two lovers is not permanent. Love transcends geographies, cultures, and subcultures. Love is universal. Love is the definition of the Divine. The contextual reference of love is generally person-to-person. There are other dimensions of love—love for the transcendent spirit, love of nature, love for self-enrichment—that are beyond the focus of this discussion.

Stories like *Romeo and Juliet* continue to remain quintessential tearjerkers because they evoke the powerful emotion of true love. It's the power of love that generates the familiar vibration in our soul—butterflies in the stomach, the skipping of a heartbeat, flushing of the face, and tears of joy are all expressions of this vibration. Scientists attribute this to hormones like oxytocin and neurotransmitters like serotonin. Despite the factual accuracy behind this science, the mystery and poetry of love is completely lost when one reduces this amazing experience to chemical names. Rabindranath Tagore pens the enigma of the mysterious love through his poetry in the collection called *Stray Birds*: "In the moon thou sendest thy love letters to me," said the night to the sun. "I leave my answers in tears upon the grass." It is those tears that the sun soaks up with its warmth. If this is not true love, then what is?

I am convinced that love is the singular potion that has the transformative powers to remove much of the darkness from our lives and close *The Gap* between the source of love and our conscious being. Most will attest to the intoxicating spell that love can cast on our mind, body, and soul. But in order for it to be the true love our soul seeks, it must be born of humility and of gratitude and not from one's ego. It must have a spiritual nature for it to have a durable future. And this love must be complete and not selective. Like a flower, it loves the fragrance just as much as it loves the thorns that protect it from predators; it loves its petals as much as it loves the color that makes them sparkle with life; it loves the rain that sometimes alters it beauty as much as the breeze that makes it dance; it loves the sun that scorches its skin as much as the soil that feeds its soul. A flower loves totally and completely. The reason it does is because it knows how to give its love selflessly, without even a hint of ego. It gives its beauty, fragrance, freshness, and brightness to any and all. In contrast, most of us allow our ego to express itself in a form that *appears* to be love flowering in our bosom. Because love is intimately intertwined with ego, it is equally addictive and mind-numbing.

If love is so powerful and magical, then let's address the natural question: why is it also so fragile? Why do we fall in love and then fall out of love, sometimes faster than we can spell l-o-v-e? Why do we end up separating from someone we once loved dearly? How does a feeling that felt so permanent and so divine lose its magic over time? It's rather simple to understand.

Wikipedia, arguably not the most definitive but still a relevant source of information today, suggests that the phrase *falling in love* may be problematic because "... the use of the term 'fall' implies that the process is in some way uncontrollable and risky—as in the phrases 'to fall ill' or 'to fall into a trap'—and that leaves the lover in a state of vulnerability." I agree. Isn't this description the exact opposite of what we expect from love? Perhaps being vulnerable and uncontrollable is an exciting part of initially falling in love, but that's not what we want love to look like forever. We seek love for security, not vulnerability; to find reward, not risk; to be in control, not out of control.

Despite its fragility, love is that primal feeling, that natural force that has the power to unite us with our Inner Self, our soul. Because love *is* our soul. That's why love arrives unannounced and overwhelms us. Our soul does not rest and cannot rest until it finds the love it felt in the womb of the Creator. We lose our appetite, we cannot sleep, we smile for no reason, we ache for our lover, and our friends can tell when love has overpowered our being. We cannot get enough of our lover; we want to be with that person at all times. The yearning to unite with that individual is so overpowering that all reason fails against love's might. This feeling is pure and fills us with divine music. It's like a melodious tune filling a hollow flute. The sweet music of love transcends everything. We can feel the Creator and His magic when we are in love. We become hypnotized by its power and are intoxicated by its promise. We want to keep it at any cost. Isn't that why a broken heart hurts so much for so long when this magic slips away unexpectedly? Even the mere thought of separation from our beloved brings back the deep-seated memory of the separation from our Inner Self at birth. Unfortunately, the only way society has taught us to "secure" what's ours and to stake our claim on it is through legally and socially accepted ceremonies like marriage. So, some lovers date while some live together before legitimizing their exclusive bond with matrimony.

Sooner or later, lovers realize that the music of love is slipping away. Our pride, our ego, and our sense of independence start getting in the way of the delicate fragrance of love until the sacred bond fractures. Some use phrases like "we grew apart," "the fire was gone," "it wasn't fun anymore," "there was no joy left in our relationship," "there was no passion," or "we were simply not in love any more." While some are able to keep the music alive by keeping the notes fresh; others are exhausted by this effort. They feel a strange knot inside when their lover expresses any degree of possessiveness, jealousy, suspicion, or other negative feelings that challenge our independence, our pride, and our ego.

We abhor being a slave to anything or to anyone because at our core, our consciousness is free and unbound. Feelings of becoming someone else's "possession" are nothing but thorns around the delicate flower of love. Somewhere inside us we begin to suspect that what we called love may have been a need for security—just like any other physical possession. Once trust in love is lost, our partner's words become like thorns. We begin viewing them through the lens of doubt and even disdain. Eventually, thorns become bigger and start hurting us. Our focus shifts away from the flower and its fragrance, and all we see and feel are the thorns. Even during this spiraling emotional whirlpool, we might still smell the beautiful fragrance of love that once was, and we yearn for it again. We try, but the vision of the flower's beauty starts to fade as the dust from our daily life gathers over it.

A realization takes root inside us that what we called love was more of the same—a transient feeling of joy that started disappearing soon after marriage. We realize that the mortal love we received was conditional whereas the Creator's love we once experienced was spiritual, nonbinding, and free-flowing without any expectations. Was it the marriage, a social contract of belonging that destroyed the love, or was it simply our ego, our shadow that covered it with darkness? Was it our possessiveness, jealousy, or envy that slowly eroded our love? Perhaps it was infidelity and sexual compulsion that created a deep rift of mistrust between former sweethearts. Some estimates place the figure of divorce caused by infidelity at a minimum of 50 percent. It's likely much higher since many don't disclose the cause to avoid embarrassment, family friction, or cultural rebuke.

Regardless, the wound is real and it hurts ... a lot. It causes pain because after so much effort, care, and attention, we come away betrayed and empty-handed again. Perhaps the experience makes us wiser, and we may even feel a sense of gratitude toward it. But no one can argue that heartbreak is an excruciating, inexplicably painful condition that borders on insanity, depression, and anxiety. It's a tornado of emotions. We want to scream, cry, run, and sometimes hurt ourselves to ease the pain. Nothing helps. Only time acts as an ointment to heal the wound. But the scar never goes away, even if we are lucky enough to find love again. In fact, scientific evidence shows that our memory modifies itself each time we retrieve the images of pain from our brain. So, the more we think about the heartbreak or any pain for that matter, the more it changes. The intensity of that feeling shifts over time. Hence, time becomes the most powerful healer. Once the pain has subsided enough, we are ready to find our true love once again because that's the ultimate desire of our soul. As with the first one, the new amorous interludes often turn out to be just that—interludes. Only very few find their true love, their spiritual partner, in another human being, perhaps because they act as a light for each other, thus removing each other's shadow or ego from *The Gap*.

For most of us, multiple failures in love cause the seed of resentment to grow inside as our consciousness realizes that this so-called love with another mortal being is actually pushing us away from our own soul. Continual heartbreak fills us with more darkness. The shimmering light we saw when we fell in love held the promise of removing the darkness and giving us boundless happiness. Our experience, however, confirmed that it was nothing but a mirage. It was not the humble and eternal Light that fills our life with gratitude and joy. It simply appeared to be so. Resentment grows into disappointment and disillusionment. Deep down we feel robbed of our freedom in our silent search for lasting peace and contentment, for the Creator, for our Inner Self. Separation and divorce become real possibilities.

The divide between two previous lovers becomes an expression of the frustration that signifies our failure to find eternal joy. At times this divide is so wide and ugly that we lose mutual respect and even our humanity while going through a divorce. For some, maya, or the material illusion, somehow takes front stage, and the human being we loved so dearly transforms into an enemy. Anger, hate, anxiety, and a multitude of negative emotions create a fog so thick that it blinds many with selfish rage. Once the connection with our life partner is severed, however, rage is often replaced by regret and sadness. We sought security but found vulnerability; we hoped for a reward, but risked our freedom; we desired balance and control, but life became uncontrollable. What started as a joyous ceremony in the sanctity of marriage ended up in a public display of shock, disappointment, sadness, and anger. *The Gap* becomes darker and the Light becomes distant still.

Khalil Gibran, in his book *The Prophet*, gives the secret recipe for love's survival in a lasting merger of two souls in marriage—what some have called a spiritual union:

...But let there be spaces in your togetherness, and let the winds of the heavens dance between you.

Love one another but make not a bond of love:

Let it rather be a moving sea between the shores of your souls.

Fill each other's cup but drink not from one cup.

Give one another of your bread but eat not from the same loaf.

Sing and dance together and be joyous, but let each one of you be alone.

Even as the strings of a lute are alone though they quiver with the same music...

We can hear the strings of spiritual love quivering with the same divine music in nature around us. The river and the ocean, bound in natural love by their humility and gratitude, know how to sing and dance together and be joyous. Once together, they become inseparable and in perfect harmony with each other. The butterfly's love affair with flowers; dewdrops kissing the flower petals; birds singing to the sun at sunrise; ocean caressing the beauty of the silent sky in its bosom; clouds playing hide-and-seek with the moon; stars twinkling happily at each other; leaves dancing as the breeze kisses them gently; earth expressing its gratitude through its fragrance when rain falls on its parched breast are all examples of divine love songs all around us. We simply need to understand its spiritual nature so our love for another sentient being can flourish too.

Love, only as the river knows, is not anywhere else but in her own spirit—in her sacrifice, song, freshness, purity, humility, gratitude, and in her aching desire to give up control and lose herself in her true lover—the ocean. Her soul already knows how to find the ocean, even if it is thousands of miles away from its glacial origin. Her final resting place is simply a representation of the refuge of love. With clouds reflecting in her soul and nature's song in her bosom, the river is love itself. She does not seek love, it naturally moves to merge with it selflessly. The eternal union of her true spirit with her Creator, the ocean, is devoid of the desire to hold on to her own identity. In fact, she wants to lose herself completely, so she can unite with her spiritual partner in the tranquil recesses of the ocean. That's when love becomes divine and permanent.

Most humans seem incapable of such a perfect union because our love is often clouded by our shadow—our ego. If we seek and desire true love, we must come out of our own shadow and embrace humility, gratitude, compassion, and understanding. We must acknowledge and honor our partner's soul and support her in this spiritual journey. Pierre Teilhard de Chardin, a French philosopher, understood this perfectly when he wrote, "We are not human beings having a spiritual experience. We are spiritual beings having a human experience." If we recognize the truth in this statement, then shedding our ego will be a small price to pay for such a big prize—finding our spiritual lover. We will not only become capable of eternal love for others, but we will be able to love ourselves completely.

Rabindranath Tagore yearned for the same as he expressed his thirst in these beautiful lines:

Not for me is the love that knows no restraint and is like foaming wine that, having burst its vessel in a moment, would run to waste.

Send me the love that is cool and pure like Your rain, which blesses the thirsty earth and fills the homely earthen jars.

Send me the love that would soak down into the center of being, and from there would spread like the unseen sap through the branching tree of life, giving birth to fruits and flowers.

Send me the love that keeps the heart still with the fullness of peace.

Such pure love and sexuality are closely linked. Science has removed much of the mystery and magic from the poetry of thinkers like Rabindranath Tagore and Khalil Gibran. The all-powerful feeling that at times blinds us to reason has now been scientifically shown as essentially a physiological process. Testosterone and estrogen are credited with the first stage of love—lust and physical attraction. As love progresses and sexual activity between lovers becomes more frequent, neurotransmitters like dopamine and serotonin become dominant in our bloodstream and stimulate the pleasure centers of our brain. Couples begin to "fall in love" as these neurotransmitters do their magic. Psychologists can now explain all the cuddling, focused attention, and exquisite delight that lovers experience simply by measuring the release of these neurotransmitters and hormones. As love "matures," fewer and fewer quantities of these chemicals are released, which explains falling out of love. One day, we may find these elements in the pharmacy so we can fall in love and stay in love forever. That would be a blissful moment in itself!

Since these chemicals activate the same area of the brain as the one that gets stimulated in addicts who are shackled by substances like cocaine, LSD, and other drugs, love can become an addiction. In fact, love and sex addiction are now well recognized by psychologists. There are rehab clinics offering "cleansing and recovery" for love and sex addicts. Sex and Love Addicts Anonymous has created a 12-step recovery program for those afflicted by this addiction. Sex and love, therefore, are intimate, inseparable partners. While loveless sex is often associated with feelings of sin and even labeled as such by some religions, sex filled with love feels like a divine union. The two can often get confused.

The Traditional View: Love and marriage have formed the traditional bonds between two people since time immemorial. While love is a pure human condition, marriage is simply a social bond that two people create so they can feel "secure" in their togetherness. This is a way of declaring to the world that two people belong to each other. Ironically, it's the same belonging that breeds the feeling of possessiveness that eventually creates all kinds of complications and makes the music of love start to wane. In fact, if you consider the origin of marriage, it was not created to "capture" your loved one. As early as 20,000 years ago, marriages were simply an efficient system to procreate, handle property rights, and protect the bloodlines. It was about self-preservation. Love was not the primary catalyst. Only later did marriage and love become natural partners.

While some cultures shun even the thought or talk of divorce, other societies seem to have plenty of it. The low divorce rate in some cultures may not tell the whole story of ugly cracks below an apparently normal or even "happy" marriage. As an East Indian, I know firsthand the taboo around divorce, especially for women. Until recently, it was extremely difficult, if not impossible, for a divorced woman in India to remarry. In fact, Eastern society always blamed the woman for the failure of marriage. Rumors that she cannot bear a child or that she is promiscuous promised to malign her reputation among family and friends. She would be considered "free and available" only for men's sexual pleasures if she were to divorce. Her treatment would be similar to someone who is excommunicated from the religion for having committed sins. Perhaps worse. While an excommunicated person has other options, a divorced woman in these cultures has nowhere to go. Even her parents sometimes refuse to give her the shelter in a place she once called home.

The visions of such a shameful life prevented women from seeking divorce, even if they lived in an extremely abusive environment. Bride burning, or the act of punishing the woman by setting her on fire for her family's failure to meet the groom's demands for dowry, is the most despicable form of abuse that some women endured and still do in some parts of India. The ancient practice of sati, in which the widow was burned alive on the funeral pyre of her dead husband, was an ugly reflection of a widowed woman's status in society. While the Indian Supreme Court has banned the practice, one still hears reports of such terrible customs that degrade not only the human being but also the soul that lives inside us all. So, a low divorce rate in a society is not necessarily a reflection of successful marriages. Something ugly and deeply disturbing can hide behind the dark shadows of those artificially low numbers.

In a society that encourages independent thought and action, divorce is commonplace. It is not unusual to find divorce rates that exceed fifty percent in the Western world, where children are reared with a sense of pride in their independence. High divorce rates are not necessarily bad because they allow two people to try another chance at life and happiness, as elusive as it may prove again. However, divorce can cause serious psychological damage among couples and children, especially if the divorce is "ugly." Couples might engage in therapy and try to make it work, but for some the divide between two egos or ideologies is far too great and divorce becomes inevitable. Some call it fate, some kismet, some divine intention. Once again, we attribute the cause of our failure in love and marriage to external forces, to maya, without truly looking inward. That's where many of us miss an amazing opportunity to grow spiritually.

The Wah! Perspective: The irony in marriage and divorce is one of love. Generally speaking, well-intentioned love for the other brings two people together in marriage, while misguided love for the self (ego) breaks the bond of marriage. The initiating party to divorce is often labeled selfish, and the other is generally labeled the victim. The definitions of selfish and victim imply the presence of ego in both parties. Does it really matter whose ego is selfish and whose is the victim? The end result is the same because both are steeped in darkness—one in pride and the other in pity. And the real victims who get lost in this darkness, some forever, are the children.

There's enough psychological evidence of the dark effects caused by two people who break the social bond because love has gone out of their lives. The desire to live happily but separately sometimes has the exact opposite effect on children, especially very young ones and adolescents up to the age of thirteen. Young children tend to become regressive and can be overcome by anxiety about their own future as they are shuttled between two households. It is not uncommon to see them regress to wetting their beds and having temper tantrums because they are trying to get the attention of the two parents in the hope that they may come back together. All they want is for the family unit that was once their safe harbor to be whole again. Adolescents, on the other hand, tend to display a more aggressive behavior with rebellion and show of independence. Once again, the bedrock of trust and love that held the family together has been shattered. For an adolescent, it is time to figure out life on her own since she cannot depend on the family unit anymore.

The darkness of a breakup between two people who had once professed love for each other and had united in body and soul can shatter young children's and adolescents' view of life. While it is natural to feel compassion for the children and the perceived "victim" of divorce, it's harder to feel the same way for the "selfish" party who is deemed to be the cause of the break-up. However, karunā is universal because it is focused on the soul. It does not discriminate or try to assign blame. It simply tries to understand and see the soul that's suffering behind the darkness regardless of whether it's that of the victim, the children, or the selfish parent. All members of the family are trying to do their best to get to the same place—they all want to be peaceful and happy. The only difference is that society views and judges their actions differently. And it shapes the views of all parties involved in a divorce. While the pain experienced is very personal, it is triggered more by the perceived shift of our place in society.

"How will I explain this to my parents/friends/colleagues?" or "Why is this happening to our family? All others around us are living a normal life." Or "Why is God punishing us?" Endless questions plague us because we live in a society that, for the most part, finds the concept of divorce troubling. A simple filter of karunā can provide a humble answer.

Children may be too young to understand the concept of karunā, especially when they are in the early developmental stage and are experiencing divorce in the family. However, every adult has an infinite capacity to express compassion and loving-kindness for others. It's the Creator's boundless gift to us. Leaving the reason for divorce aside, it is important to recognize that all members of the family need empathy, understanding, and large doses of karunā. They are all expressing their yearning to find happiness. If they cannot find common ground, they behave in a different manner and assume different directions. At times, marriage counselors, family members, religious leaders, and community members are able to bring the family back together. Sometimes all efforts fail. Even those who are engaged in this service to bring amity and compromise are seeking the same—a feeling of peace that's felt when we can help others reach a peaceful place. Light begets Light.

So, karunā can become the bedrock for possible healing, even if the differences between two married people cannot be reconciled. It is karunā that can bring hope to the affected children, and it is karunā for each other that can allow the parents to heal. Perhaps most important is not just compassion for each other but compassion for oneself. The field of "mindful divorce" is fast taking hold as a mechanism to bring compassion to this terrible human condition. Mindfulness can help bring understanding and appreciation for the other, without judgment. The result can be relative peace and a possibility of a new beginning without the social bond of marriage. Perhaps a relationship without such a bond has a better chance at thriving because there's lesser friction of egos. That allows for room for understanding, compassion, and love to grow again. This love may look different, but it's likely to be more durable.

In addition to karunā and love, children still need what psychologists call the three "R's"—routines, rituals, and reassurance. Life doesn't have to be perfect. Like they say, perfect is the enemy of good. Perhaps, the easiest way to find karunā in our hearts during this difficult process is to understand one of the most destructive emotions—anger—whose fury can leave a blazing trail of destruction behind.

8

anger's wrath

"The soul is like a bowl of water, the external impressions like the ray of light falling upon the water. If the water is agitated, it appears that the light itself is disturbed too, but that is not so. So, when a person loses their tranquility it isn't their knowledge and virtues that are disturbed, but the spirit in which they exist, and when that spirit settles down so do the knowledge and virtues."

—Epictetus, Discourses

I have many pleasant memories of my childhood like most children do. However, these memories are interspersed with some deeply troubling flashes of life at home. One evening in particular is permanently etched in my brain when my father, in his utter frustration and dejection, completely destroyed our small but sacred shrine at home. He had completely lost faith in God that evening because none of his efforts were producing any results and he could not care for his family the way any father would like to. While it was terrifying to witness the fury of his anger as a child, it is only now that I can understand his mental state. Clearly, he was filled with the darkness of hopelessness. Anger of that magnitude can be extremely corrosive for everyone involved, especially the person who is gripped by its clutches.

Buddha famously said, "Holding on to anger is like grasping a hot coal with the intent of throwing it at someone; you are the one who gets burned." Just look at a volcano—its fury scars its own beautiful body leaving permanent scars of lava flow. Its angry eruptions of a few days or weeks cause so much damage that it takes decades for secondary forests and foliage to return, if ever. My father, while an incredibly compassionate and loving man, had a side to him that our entire household feared. His angry outbursts created an environment of fear and unpredictability at home. Sometimes his rage led to physical destruction and dark moods that lasted for days. Eventually, it was the destructive blows of anger that contributed to his illness and death. While the hot coal caused some scalding in the family, it was my father who got completely burned by it. Fearing that history may repeat itself through me, I begged God to eradicate every seed of anger from my being. I am not there yet, but the simple recognition of this destructive emotion is helping me to keep its seeds at bay, even in some of the most trying situations. It doesn't always work, but the episodes are fewer, shorter, and they leave me with a better understanding of how not to let this weed take over the garden. There's a reason why: I have had the opportunity to learn and understand its origin and its nature.

If you closely examine and observe the emotions related to anger, you will likely notice three things. First, the severity of your anger will diminish with time, and its destructive energy is generally replaced by regret and sadness, especially if you let the rage overpower you. Hence, the advice of the wise to wait for twenty-four hours before reacting to anything that upsets you. Second, you will find that anger is not an inherent part of your human nature—its trigger lies in things outside your control. And finally, a child who has not yet developed a sense of self or ego does not experience the emotion of anger as adults do—hence, a child's purity in her smile sends a wave of calm and joy through the observer.

There are some natural conclusions one can draw from these common observations. Anger is not an emotion that is embedded in our gene code. It arrives after we are born. It's absent in an innocent child. Temper tantrums in a child are just that—tantrums or an innocent display of temper given the limited vocabulary a child possesses to express her frustration. Temper and anger, while sometimes loosely used as synonyms, differ markedly in degree of severity and expression. Anger is an outcome of something that happened to us on our way to developing our sense of self. Have you ever seen a baby looking at you with angry eyes or an expression of rage and fury? Never! It's impossible because it's not in the baby's nature. It would be hilarious if we were to witness such a situation. In fact, even babies of ferocious animals cannot display the emotion of anger. Anger, therefore, is purely an external phenomenon the seeds of which are embedded in us after our birth. Since anger is not part of a child's true nature, all that a child can do is attract attention to its basic needs by doing the only thing she knows—cry or throw fits. That's not anger. It's a form of communication to the caretaker that the child needs something. Once the need is addressed, crying is replaced by giggles and bright smiles. Anger in more mature human beings dissipates similarly but over a longer period of time. Unless it entrenches itself with deep roots or explodes violently, anger generally subsides with time regardless of whether our "need" was met or the trigger that caused the anger was removed. It naturally dissolves and is replaced by calmness, regret, or a mix of other emotions. If we wait long enough, anger's energy simply transforms into something totally different, something far more peaceful and deep than the shallow restlessness.

To be sure, anger is not all bad. In fact, certain forms of anger, psychologists agree, could be essential to survival. Social scientists point out the advantages of anger that can lead to social justice and correction of wrong behaviors. Mahatma Gandhi and

Dr. Martin Luther King will disagree with these social scientists because of their unshakable belief in peaceful conduct and peaceful resolutions. Clearly, anger is viewed as a negative emotion more broadly because it is proven to not only cause harm to our body and to our mental stability but to others who are at the receiving end, especially young children. For the purpose of this text, we are concerned with the betterment of the human condition by transforming what is undesirable. Therefore, we will consider anger an adverse emotion because it hampers the pursuit of peace and love—it's opposite form of energy.

So, the question is where does anger come from, and how did it become so universal among the human race? How did we go from the state of being a peaceful child to an adult whose blood pressure and restlessness during fits of anger rival angry waves during a ferocious storm?

Psychotherapist Michael C. Graham states that anger almost always results when we were " ... expecting the world to be different than it is." The American Psychological Association defines anger as "an emotion characterized by antagonism toward someone or something you feel has deliberately done you wrong." Due to my father's misfortunes in business, his anger may seem justified in light of this definition. He felt that the entire world was against him and had done him wrong. When his actions are viewed through this narrow lens, he was right, even though, in retrospect, how he handled it in his personal life produced undesirable effects. I only wish his peaceful moments would have lasted much longer because that would have allowed us to become emotionally closer. Perhaps, I could have told him how much I loved him despite all his perceived shortcomings. Anger took that opportunity away from us.

Osho considers anger and peaceful feelings to be two sides of the same coin. It's the same energy manifesting itself in different forms. I tend to agree with Osho's and Michael Graham's analysis since we consciously decide what to do with our energy, and how and where to channel it. I believe that anger is the outward expression of its close cousins—anxiety, fear, and depression. Some psychologists agree with this assessment. My father's frequent and, at times, severe bouts of depression certainly are in line with such an assessment.

While the physiological effects of anger all point to harmful effects to our physical and mental health, interestingly, the cognitive effects of anger are actually described in positive terms. For example, studies show that angry people are likely to be more optimistic about the future; they view risks more positively and find that unfortunate situations are less likely to occur. They are also reckless risk takers because they are inherently optimistic about the outcome. My father fit this definition almost perfectly. He believed that "placing all your eggs in one basket" was a good thing because it allowed one to focus intensely and to succeed in life. The results proved otherwise. But when you place angry risk takers in a group setting, others are less likely to trust them, and they view them in a negative light. How can we explain this duality—the same emotion causing two opposite effects in the observer and the observed?

Let's examine the observer first with the reasonable assumption that, at our core, we all desire and seek peace. Anger threatens this basic peace-seeking premise, and it should not come as a surprise to anyone that we, therefore, view the emotion associated with anger negatively. Anger can also create fear and anxiety in the observer or the person on the receiving end. Scientists have observed that the amygdala, the almond-shaped region in the human brain that processes emotions like fear and anxiety, lights up when a person experiences feelings of angst and dread. Such emotions create undesirable physiological and psychological reactions that are strangely reminiscent of how a baby must have felt at birth. Anger, therefore, brings out in the observer the deeply buried, but easily accessible feelings of distress, despair, anxiety, and helplessness associated with separation at birth from our Inner Self, our higher truth.

When we consider the person who is exhibiting anger, it is likely an expression of the extreme frustration caused by repeated disappointment in finding peace and lasting love. Even after following the prescription for happiness and joy—the undaunted pursuit of material wealth and comforts—we come out empty-handed regardless of whether we achieve material success or not. The repetitive nature of this disillusionment and frustration causes some of us to carry the baggage of grievance and anger for a very long time. In order to understand the state of mind of this person, we have to compassionately understand the genesis of anger.

From childhood we are conditioned for "success," as defined by those entrusted with our care and growth. To be sure, years of such habituated growth bring maturity, intelligence, and accumulated knowledge. But all of the so-called advancement is nothing more than borrowed information derived from books and knowledge from others. Very little, if any, is unique or new. Therefore, it's not fresh and invigorating. Most of us feel compelled to use these borrowed assets to achieve success. In today's world, that means material wealth, status, position, power, outward appearance or maya. Society tells us, and we come to believe it, that if we achieve this success, we will attain happiness. So, we work hard every day to achieve these dreams. Either our hard work pays off and we achieve the American Dream, or we continue to struggle financially. In both situations, we find ourselves just as naked and empty inside as we were before we went on this conquest. It fails to bring us to the

Promised Land. Seeds of frustration get sowed, and repeated failures act as nourishment for these seeds to sprout into angry branches. These branches may appear rich and full of life or they may be poor and barren; anger is still running deep in their veins.

On one end is poverty, sometimes extreme, and on the other are all the riches the world can offer. Both accumulate disappointment in absence of our union with the Creator. All the glitter and riches can't buy us the happiness we seek so desperately. It's not surprising that many who have purportedly achieved enviable material success and fame are paraded in tabloids and news magazines with unenviable headlines. Many of them become addicted to drugs, sex, depressive behaviors, anxiety, and panic attacks. Some even reach the extreme emotional state and sadly succumb to it—Kurt Cobain, Whitney Houston, and Marilyn Monroe among countless others.

We can empathize with them because none of us are immune to this repeated disappointment. At some point in our lives, we may have felt the same pain albeit to a lesser degree. My father felt it in its worst form. He too was plagued by financial and health challenges that I am sure left him feeling inadequate as a father, husband, and friend. Eventually, this disappointment and frustration displayed its ugly head through trigger-happy anger, domestic violence, severe depression, and eventually suicide. I could not understand his actions for over twenty-five years and blamed myself for his death all these years. Now I know it was *The Gap,* the deep chasm filled with the darkness of disappointment, anxiety, anger, and hopelessness that did not allow him to be at peace, to see the Light so he could commune with his own soul. I now understand how helpless and lonely he must have felt, why anger was a common outlet for his frustration, and why anxiety and depression were close cousins to his anger.

So, whether or not we acknowledge it or recognize it, our consciousness knows that the path of success we had been following from our early days in school to adulthood was taking us farther away from the desired peace and tranquility. We were shown a way by society, and we followed it diligently. But peace and happiness still eluded us. Disappointment started to envelop us. Any external stimulus that even remotely challenged who we are as a person or the convictions we had developed acted as a flash point to light up our amygdala with a plethora of emotions that destroyed our peace.

We were already frustrated by the results, or lack thereof, of our efforts to find happiness through material comforts. And then someone or something deliberately does us wrong. Repeatedly! Expletives and almost alien body language overpowers us, and anger boils over. Or we resort to the other extreme, and anxiety, panic attacks, and depression become our refuge. This self-sustaining loop, if not checked in time, sometimes becomes uncontrollable and leads to terrible consequences. The thick fog of anger has the power to completely obliterate the image of our pure, serene soul. The transient and hollow warmth of maya is powerless in clearing this fog.

And The Gap darkens yet again. Our Higher Self—the embodiment of ultimate peace and serenity—is pushed farther away from us. Initially, the darkness present in our own depths may frighten us. Our inability to traverse these depths may give rise to a conviction that our depths do not harbor any tranquility. Hence, we wade on the surface, afraid of the dark depths, completely unaware that the light we see on the surface is an illusion.

However, the stories of those who have successfully accessed the bliss residing in their own depths—mortals like Buddha, Guru Nanak, Jesus, Lao Tzu—give us comfort and assurance that there is a path to the higher ground where there's Light. It simply passes through the valley of darkness. Anger is the superficial restless representation of our yearning to remove this darkness. It is the same energy that harbors peace and tranquility in its bosom, just like the restless waves that are not separate from the peaceful sanctuary of the ocean.

Many of us understand that darkness and light coexist in our being. The fact that we can see this darkness means that there's light around it and behind it. Our source of light is the

Light of the Creator, the Light of our consciousness, the Light of our awareness, dulled as it may have become over time. Anger has simply obscured the Light. All we have to do to allow the Light to shine on us is to remove this sphere of rage so we can become luminous once again. For some, this blessed moment arrives early in life and for others much later, even as we are fading away. Nonetheless, we can be like the hot sun that spreads its warmth and beauty even as it sets below the horizon.

The Traditional View: The traditional view that informs our attitudes toward anger is influenced by the daily grind of life. When we are living our life intensely, there's little time to reflect. We are too busy accumulating the illusory maya. We are too occupied with our quest to reach the island called happiness. Anger is the defense mechanism to keep us focused on this mission.

In fact, the French psychoanalyst and psychiatrist Jacques Lacan theorized that anger or aggression is a defense mechanism against what he called "fragmentation." Dr. Lacan argued that during childhood we are a jumble of different biological processes, and we lack a coherent identity. When we do pull it all together during adulthood, our identity is still an illusion. It is a veil that hides our vulnerabilities and weaknesses. If challenged, we try hard not to expose these weaknesses, and we use aggression or anger to ward off the threat of exposure. We want to create the same illusion among others about our identity—that we are a coherent whole. If we are honest with ourselves, we can all relate to Dr. Lacan's theory about aggression and anger.

Many of us have raised the middle finger, shouted obscenities, or blown our horn loudly when someone has violated our right of way, whether it was while driving a car on a busy road or in other walks of life. In fact, any time we experience such a violation, physiological responses in our body create a chain of events that lead to the psychological response of aggression. Some of these aggressive responses come out immediately while others remain repressed and can cause much graver damage to our own mental and physical health and to that of others over time. In a direct response, we intend to cause harm to someone who hurt us. And at times, this harm is indirectly turned inward and causes feelings of guilt and leads to depression.

Traditional psychology and viewpoints simply see anger as a dark force that is intended to cause harm to those who may have hurt us. None of the science-based modalities of dealing with this dark force acknowledge the spirituality behind it. Anger is dealt with at its face value as a negative force that must be eliminated with reason and logic so that calm can prevail. Even Hollywood has been infatuated with this issue and has produced blockbuster comedies like *Anger Management*. While such methods may work, they are only temporary solutions since they do not address the core issues behind this darkness. They are like Band-Aids applied on deep wounds that may stop them from bleeding, but don't fully heal the wounds. So, rather than just fixing the symptoms and pruning the destructive branches, a better approach may be to stop watering the seeds of anger altogether.

The Wah! Perspective: The seeds of anger, if not checked and transformed, can overwhelm our beautiful garden of life with weeds of heartache, despair, anxiety, illness, and even suicide. Anger is a superficial force learned after birth and, as such, it has no connection with our soul. Even psychology recognizes that anger is a veil to shield our vulnerabilities and weaknesses. Anger is darkness that covers our pure soul, not just our vulnerabilities. Anger is bullying in its ugly form that can lead to physical, emotional, and sexual abuse. Anger is, at times, pure evil. It is difficult to come to terms with actions that are catalyzed by anger. If someone hurts us, we want revenge or we recede into a dark emotional abyss. It's a vicious spiral with dire consequences for everyone involved in its fury—the aggressor and the receiver alike. Anger is absolute darkness.

If we adopt the *We are human* or the *Wah!* perspective, we can indeed see past all the deep divides and find the rays of light that give us hope. The *Wah!* perspective presumes that despite our mortal shortcomings, we all harbor the same energy, the same purity in our bosom. We all ache to be united with our soul, our higher consciousness. We all yearn to be peaceful and not angry. Even in revenge, we seek peace by "getting even." Clearly, that's our ego taking control of our actions and blinding our view of the sublime, the pure Inner Self.

Rage is powerful and may make us believe, as misguided as the belief may be, that it can destroy the source of our unhappiness. What we don't realize is that rage is unhappiness wearing the garb of aggression. Rage is a very thick fog that can only be dissipated permanently with the warm light of compassion, empathy, and love. A simple loving hug can do miracles to destroy even the deepest form of anger. If we develop this compassion toward the aggressor, we will not only bring peace to the one experiencing rage, but a strange sense of peace will prevail in us also. The most powerful technique to quell anger is for the person experiencing this emotion to call a time-out, find compassion in his or her heart to understand the source of anger, wait for twenty-four hours and be pleasantly surprised that the seed of anger has gone dormant. If not checked, this strong emotion can lead to serious illness, suicide, and death. I know this fact firsthand.

9

illness, suicide, and death

Body and soul are like the rose and its fragrance; the rose may wither away, but the fragrance lives on, selflessly spreading its love!

When I was in my final year of college, one of my freshman friends committed suicide. He was found hanging from a ceiling fan—a common way to commit suicide in India. The news sent a shockwave throughout the college campus because he was an extremely jubilant, physically fit, and affable fellow who always had a ready smile on his face—the kind of person one would never associate with an act of such magnitude. I vividly remember the pain in his parents' and siblings' eyes. The whole scene is etched just as deeply in my mind as the day my father committed suicide. Both were hot days of summer. While my father's death was up close and personal, my friend's passing was in some ways more troubling. He was my peer. His parents had to cremate him. Life was not supposed to work like this. We are supposed to perform the last rites for our parents and not the other way around.

There were many unanswered questions around my friend's death. Was he jilted in love? Was he facing some challenges at home? Did he commit a serious crime? Did he have a terminal illness? Surprisingly, mental disease or depression never crossed our minds. During the early '80s in India, depression was simply considered a mood disorder, not a mental disease. There was no awareness about disorders of the mind. We assumed that the cause of a grave action such as suicide was in the external environment and not a part of our DNA or biological chemistry or mental design.

It's for the same reason that I have carried the guilt for over two decades that I was the cause of my father's suicide, not his mental illness. He died because I was going to commit a sin; or perhaps I did not try hard enough to care for him during his illness; or may be I did not perform CPR on him for long enough; or simply that I wished he was dead because my mother used to wish the same during her darkest days of domestic abuse. I know she loved him dearly, but anger, frustration, and despair can make people say things that are illogical, cold, and repulsive. I loved my mother greatly, and I wanted her to be happy and peaceful. As an adolescent and a teenager, her words of despair echoed in my mind all the time. Maybe it was that silent, evil, and hateful wish, despite my deep love for my father, that convinced God to end his life. After all, my mother also used to say; "God can change the world for one disciple ... " I was surely one of His ardent disciples because my mother always told me so. After all, I shared the same date of birth as one of the revered Sikh gurus.

I now believe that the primary cause of suicide and other serious psychological ailments is fragmentation of our soul. Psychologists use logic and reasoning to explain our mental illness, but the root cause is post-psychological, in my opinion. It is embedded in our spiritual being over time as life's events cause our soul to fracture. Such splintering at our spirit level can modify our behavior because we, at some level, recognize the fissures in our soul. What results from such recognition are challenges around self-love, self-esteem, shame, and guilt. While treatments like cognitive behavioral therapy and even some medications can help modify our behaviors at the psychological level, the results are often temporary or need lifetime intervention by therapists and psychiatrists. We all know the ill side effects of medications that are used to treat such conditions. Unfortunately, most of these treatments fail to recognize and acknowledge that the fragmentation has occurred at the level of our soul. It is only in the past few years, with passionate efforts of pioneers like Dr. Lisa Miller at the Spirituality Mind Body Institute (SMBI) at Columbia University, that the field of psychology is using scientific tools to better understand the mysteries of spirituality. There is hope around the corner that we may finally be able to understand core issues like disillusionment that defy scientific logic and reasoning.

However, deep disillusionment can, at times, lead to enlightenment. It is a well-known fact that Buddha's observation of the physical decline of the human body was a catalyst in the mental shift that took him from the comforts of a palace to the dangers of the forest. He was completely disillusioned about life and wanted to understand its deeper truth. He observed the transient and impermanent nature of the human body's beauty, how it was affected by disease and old age, and how it eventually became lifeless. He asked the very basic question, why are we here if we are to eventually disintegrate and disappear? Thus began his search for the meaning of life and the eternal truth. His trials and tribulations are well documented in globally popular works, from fables like Herman Hesse's *Siddhartha* to the many books of wisdom on Buddhism. Developmental psychologists like Dr. Erik Erikson have coined terms like "ego integrity," which signifies the desire to understand the meaning of life, especially as one gets older. Gautama Buddha had attained ego integrity that eventually led to his enlightenment and changed how the world thought about God and religion. Not everyone who achieves ego integrity is that fortunate, according to Dr. Erikson.

Buddha was perhaps not the first who was disturbed by the concept of aging, illness, and death. The subject has occupied man's mind for as long as we have lived. Mythological accounts of Eastern religions like Hinduism, which dates back thousands of years, and more recent scriptures like the Guru Granth Sahib, which are about 500 years old, have all addressed illness and mortality.

Despite our understanding of its inevitability, the mere thought of illness and death evokes feelings of anxiety, sadness, helplessness, and pessimism. In fact, people fear death more than anything else, even though some argue that public speaking ranks right up there! In fact death anxiety is a documented psychological concept. German philosopher Martin Heidegger has written about the "indeterminate nature of death"—that one never knows how and when one is going to die. He believed that the awareness of the fact that we will cease to exist one day, combined with the lack of knowledge of how and when we will die creates a complex and deep level of anxiety in many of us. Heidegger was a little late to espouse this theory because this sentiment was already recorded in the Sikh scriptures over 500 years ago in a verse *"Kyaa jaana kiv marenge kaisa marnaa hoye"* which means, "We don't know how we will die and what death will be like."

Religiosity, or the degree of religion's presence in one's life, has been shown to reduce death anxiety in people who are highly religious and regularly attend religious services. Some argue that it is the fear of death, in fact, that makes people more religious and not religion that makes people less fearful about dying. In a similar cause-and-effect study, William James, the prominent American psychologist, showed that it is not fear that causes the flight response. It is, in fact, the flight response that induces fear. Put simply, it's not fear that makes us run when we encounter a scary situation; it is because we run that we become fearful. Perhaps Seneca, a Roman Stoic philosopher, knew this fact intuitively since he penned it in the Latin play *Oedipus* in 992 A.D., "Many are harmed by fear itself, and many may have come to their fate while dreading fate."

We fear illness not only because of its debilitating effects that can leave us powerless, helpless, and dependent but also because of its strong association with the indeterminate nature of death. Everyone has experienced or heard of serious illness turning into a terminal condition that eventually leads to death. Whether we fear suffering during the illness or death itself is a matter of depth of fear and our psychological construct. It is, however, the strong correlation between illness, the body's eventual deterioration, and death that creates fear and anxiety among us. Perhaps this was the very anxiety that motivated

Buddha to take upon his solitary journey of over twelve years before he attained enlightenment. It's the same passionate anxiety that keeps dedicated researchers awake at night to find a cure for serious illnesses and infections.

It's easy to understand why outbreaks of swine flu, mad cow disease, Ebola, and the Zika virus have caused panic in recent history. Such intensity of fear invokes undue caution, almost like a freeze response, that can cause human and economic activity to come to a screeching halt. One could argue that it is the illness of the mind that is far more crippling than the physical effects of the illness because we suffer mentally even before any illness causes physical suffering. Nothing matters more to our mind than our good health because we associate it with longevity. A longer life, we believe, improves the odds of enjoying life and finding happiness. For some, longevity may allow for a higher probability of achieving salvation, nirvana, or enlightenment. Regardless, we universally prefer a longer, healthier life as opposed to a shorter one beseeched by sickness and illness.

To try to better understand death and what happens after death, there's a whole field of study dedicated to what is called "near-death experience" or NDE, a term coined by psychiatrist and psychologist Raymond Moody in his 1975 book *Life After Life*. These experiences range from a floating feeling of peace and beauty to distressing feelings of terror and fear. People have reported NDEs when they have either come very close to death or were declared dead or were immersed in profound grief or a deep meditative state. In his famous book, *Many Lives, Many Masters,* psychiatrist Brian Weiss describes the true story of a woman who was able to recall past-life traumas that helped explain her current fears and anxieties. Despite his early reservations, he was convinced after she provided accounts from his own life that only Dr. Weiss knew to be true. These "visions" ultimately helped Dr. Weiss in treating her chronic condition. The entire experience changed two lives forever—Dr. Weiss's and that of his patient.

Death, therefore, has been a subject of curiosity, intrigue, and study in human psychology for many centuries. Once again, the bigger question is *why? Why* do we fear death? *Why* are we scared by the uncertainty surrounding death and the unknown nature of a disease that may inflict us? How can we explain that religiosity can reduce the degree of this fear if not completely erase it, as some contend?

Once again, the answer may be simpler than we expect. Illness and death are those areas of uncertainty whose true nature our logical brain fails to understand because there are no hard facts or data to explain it. There are no coordinates that one could put together for any disease, ailment, or human condition that could decipher the code to unlock the timing and nature of death. And that bothers our logical left brain ... a lot. These fears begin to sprout quite early in life. Scientific studies show that fears of all kind start to show their ugly face in children as young as four years old. If we could have infants respond to surveys and take tests that we administer to four-year-olds, we may find the evidence of such fears even among them. So why do we all fear illness and death? Why is suicide considered a sin by some religions and a cowardly act against God by others?

The Traditional View: For those who are entangled in the web of maya, it is the fear of separation from all that is material—family, friends, possessions, positions, luxuries, and comforts. It may also be the regret that we did not get to check off all the items on our bucket list—that trip to Tuscany, marrying the love of our life, having beautiful children, adopting someone, helping those in need, buying the yacht to sail the world. The list is endless and so are our entanglements. Some argue it's the concern for the wellbeing of those we leave behind when we die that brings about death anxiety. It's not unusual to see ashen faces of passengers in an airplane when it goes through sudden or sustained turbulence. We feel out of control. We feel helpless. We feel alone. We see death staring us in our face. We worry about those we may leave behind. The construct of sudden death is just as terrifying as a terminal illness that slowly eats away at our health and spirit.

Terminally ill patients typically fall into three categories: those who have hope that they will recover and become healthy again, those who passively welcome death and want to hasten its arrival, and those who actively pursue drastic action like suicide. I have personal experience with the latter two. Even though my father was not terminally ill, in his mind his life was useless. For caregivers, including doctors and family members, watching this previously healthy person whither away is one of the most painful aspects of life. It is especially difficult when the patient is on medical life-support systems and the family has to decide when to "pull the plug." Physician or family assisted euthanasia is a subject of intense moral and legal debate in many parts of the world. Frankly, it takes an immense amount of courage, humility, and loving-kindness for anyone to assist another in the passage from life to death. There's no bond more sacred and divine than the one that binds two souls together in this dance of life and death involving the one who wants to die and the one who assists in making it possible. While there's turmoil mixed with understanding and compassion in the heart of one assisting in this life-death decision, there's gratitude and love in the soul of the other who wants to make the journey to the other side. As a tangential but important remark, everyone should have a living will and advance medical directives so we don't impose the burden of this decision on our loved ones or on any of our caregivers.

The Wah! Perspective: One explanation for death anxiety could be that it is another form of separation anxiety that we discussed in the chapter *Birth of The Gap*. While illness creates the fear of separation through death, death itself is the ultimate separation. Death anxiety, therefore, is nothing but separation anxiety disguised by the darkness and the fear of death.

While separation from all that is maya is real, it is also extremely superficial. At a deeper subconscious level, death anxiety is harbored for a divine reason. The realization in our subconscious mind that we may never again get a chance to be united with our Creator is the cause of mankind's biggest fear— death. The understanding that we may never achieve what our consciousness craves—the ultimate peace and tranquility associated with the divine union with our Creator—is the foundation where death anxiety is anchored. The awareness that we may never be able to remove the darkness from *The Gap* or peel off some of the layers of dirt so that Light may reveal itself is a cause of pain and suffering, even in death and illness.

When we view the human condition of fear of illness and death through a compassionate lens, we are filled with empathy for those who are fighting terminal illness at home, in the hospital, and in hospice centers. When my mother was breathing her last breath at a local hospice, she was having a very difficult time leaving her body. The hospice nurse said to us that she is hanging on for some reason. She advised that one of us tell her that it is okay to go to the other side and reassure her that everything will be okay. My mother and sister were especially close, and my mother adored her grandchildren. I knew instinctively that it was the concern for my sister's well-being and her love for the grandchildren that was keeping her tied to this physical realm. We played hymns in her room, and we all prayed for her. I spent time talking to her and promised her that all will be fine. Soon thereafter she took her last breath. Even in death, she was fearful of death because of her attachments.

Karunā can truly help us empathize with end-of-life patients. At a mortal level, they are suffering intensely. Loss of dignity, depression, suicidal thoughts, unbearable physical pain, and a feeling of dependence on others would be unbearable suffering for anyone. At a deeper level, their soul is aching to merge with the Creator. This desired union is nothing but an illusion because our Creator is always within us—we were never separated from Him. Only those who have awakened from the deep slumber induced by maya have the ability to die in peace just as they lived in peace.

The spiritually awakened and even the highly religious feel closer to the Creator. They report a much lesser degree of death anxiety and much larger acceptance of disease as a passing phase to renew our body. Such people are also more likely to report a higher degree of humility and gratitude that, as studies have shown, can have a significant positive effect on our physical and emotional well-being.

Treatments, such as the meaning-centered psychotherapy conducted on cancer patients by Dr. William S. Brietbart, Vice Chair of Memorial Sloan Kettering's Department of Psychiatry and Behavioral Science, have shown positive results even at the end of one's life. Some scientific studies have focused on the desire in terminally ill patients to hasten their death when life seems meaningless. The results are not surprising—those who were able to connect their life with a purpose or meaning displayed significant protection against depression, desire for hastened death, and even suicidal thoughts. Spirituality was their Light even during the hours that are the darkest for most mortal beings.

Such mortals understand in the depths of their soul that, as Seneca wrote in *Moral Letters to Lucilius*, "It is not the last drop that empties the water-clock, but all that which previously has flowed out ... " They understand how precious every moment of our life is in the march toward mortality—that every drop, every breath matters. They live life with complete awareness and do so by being present to every beautiful moment that nature unveils.

Sincere gratitude fills them with humility as they are awed by the gift of life that each moment brings. It appears that such souls are ever-present to the knowledge that the chain of life may be cut abruptly or it may grind itself down to a state of fragility when it must break. Many fear this break, but those who know how to live celebrate each moment because, ironically, mortality is the fuel that lights their fire of life.

Feelings of gratitude and humility in such people lead to desirable human conditions of compassion, forgiveness, love, and inner peace. Most religions consider these "Godlike" qualities. Is it any surprise, then, that religiosity may have a dampening effect on the fear associated with death and sickness? Even atheists, who value humility and who are filled with gratitude, claim similar reduction in this anxiety. Humility and gratitude help remove the dirt and darkness from *The Gap*. Even the simple realization that there's Light behind the darkness can place us at some level of ease with the concept of illness and death. It is clear that the minds of such souls become stronger with wisdom, even as their bodies wither away against the inevitable force of nature. As I witnessed in my mother's case, prayer was her secret ingredient that gave her the strength to absorb life's tsunamis and earthquakes. It was her only weapon to fight death until her last breath.

I often wondered what was going through her mind during her last days and hours. When she did pass, our entire family was filled with a sense of loss, and each of us processed our grief differently. The common thread between us all was that the definition of family and our relationships with each other had altered forever. The immense sorrow of losing a parent, especially the second surviving parent, is especially deep and painful. Perhaps we experience the fragility of life and come face-to-face with our own mortality. We all deal with this new reality in our own unique way. For many, prayer, meditation, and a spiritual perspective offer unmatched comfort.

Surprisingly, it was a scientific story about C-14, a carbon isotope in the air, which aired on NPR that brought me a spiritual understanding about my mother's death. As the world tested atomic bombs in the 1950s, the amount of C-14 doubled in the atmosphere that was breathed in by plants that were, in turn, eaten by animals. As humans consumed the animals, C-14 ended up in our bodies and is now used by researchers to tell the age of our tissues and how often they renew themselves. This news and commentary strangely connected me with the day I offered my mother's ashes to a sacred river in India. While it was an emotionally unsettling day, the story helped me visualize the atoms of her body merging with the water that was carried by clouds to oceans far and wide, imbibed by animals quenching their thirst, and absorbed by plants that the river nourished. That's how my mother became part of the Universe once again. Now, whenever it rains, or I eat a piece of delicious fruit or vegetables or fish, I know my mom is there with me. As difficult as her death has been, it gives me strange comfort to know that I am ingesting her atoms and quenching my thirst with the water that has her spirit. She is always with me. Although it was difficult for her to let go of this mortal life, I am sure there was a part of her that knew the end was near. I am sometimes gripped by overwhelming grief when I wonder about her internal dialogue during those last hours of her life.

Rabindranath Tagore captures some of what my mother may have conversed with her God in this beautiful prayer dubbed *The Heart of God*:

I know that the day will come when my sight of this earth shall be lost, and life will take its leave in silence, drawing the last curtain over my eyes.

Yet stars will watch at night, and morning rise as before, and hours heave like sea waves casting up pleasures and pains.

When I think of this end of my moments, the barrier of moments breaks and I see by the light of death Your world with its careless treasures, Rare is its lowliest seat; rare is its meanest of lives.

Things that I longed for in vain and things that I got – let them pass. Let me but truly possess the things that I ever spurned and overlooked.

10

sorrow, grief, and despair

"Give sorrow words. The grief that does not speak whispers the o'er-fraught heart and bids it break."

—*Shakespeare, Macbeth*

Recently, my cousin passed away suddenly. I had not seen him in over a decade, but his sudden death at a young age of forty was a reminder of the fragility of life. It was also a reminder of love – that those we love can leave without notice and that we are then left with nothing but questions and remorse. When one question gets answered, new ones appear, and the healing process can take a lifetime. For me, his death was also a reminder of a love that I had forgotten—love for other members of my family who had curiously become estranged since my father's suicide.

At his funeral, the pain and suffering was so utterly raw and visible in his parents' and sister's eyes that it shook my soul to the core. The grief of losing a child or a sibling is perhaps the most numbing pain of human existence. I could feel their immense pain, as I had also experienced mortality up close and personal. I watched my aunt gaze at her son's face in the casket as if she was looking at her newborn in a crib, tears rolling down her cheeks with a faint smile on her lips. It will take a lifetime to understand the pain of this mother since her grief had its origin in the deep love for her son. Before this day, I had never seen my uncle or my cousin sister cry. That day, their tears were unstoppable. They seemed like a fish that had been thrown out of the water and whose life was being sucked away by air. A father's pride and a sister's big brother lay lifeless, and no amount of pleading or crying could now wake him up. Words cannot capture the pangs of pain that they were experiencing and the depth of grief that was afflicting them. My heart still aches thinking about that day. I only wish I could somehow absorb their pain with something as simple as a warm, familial hug since words, in such situations, are nothing but empty shells. But I know I cannot. They must endure and go through this experience in their own unique way. I can only pray that they become stronger with time.

We all have such stories—some that hit close to home and others that are a bit more distant. Stories differ but narratives are the same. Hence, the proclamation by the enlightened ones that everyone suffers. And grief is one dimension of such a suffering.

Where does the human expression of so much sorrow

originate? What is its source? I believe that we are not coded with grief while we are in our mother's womb. On the contrary, grief is not part of the vocabulary of our emotions during those serene nine months. Curiously, I believe that the first instance we experience grief is at birth. The connection with our Creator, our Higher Self, our God dies that day. Losing something so eternal and integral to our being creates a permanent marker in our psyche, and that sense of loss leads to grief. It's the grief we associate with death.

The definition of grief, according to the *Merriam-Webster Dictionary* is "deep sadness caused especially by someone's death; a cause of deep sadness." The original death, in my humble view, is the loss of the innate connection with the Supreme. Therefore, grief is probably not an experience that occurs after we develop our sense of self; it is most likely hardwired in our being at birth. It is the first fragmentation of our soul. And its genesis is in the original Light of conception.

Our mothers and other caretakers recognize and can feel this pain during our infancy, but they label it with other names like colic, hunger, irritation, pain, and other easy-to-identify markers. At some level they understand it and rush to comfort the baby, not unlike how adults gather to console someone who has lost someone or has suffered deeply due to some extraneous event. Holding closely, hugging, and caressing are all physical acts that naturally mimic the womb or our mother's warm bosom that gave us comfort in the early months and years of our life. Absent such physical contact, we naturally regress into a fetal position during periods of extreme distress and grief as if to replicate our safe harbor in the womb where nothing could hurt us.

I recall when I was lying in such a position during a gloomy but introspective day at a meditation camp in Florida. As I got up, I noticed the ocean was in a similar state of distress and restlessness. I sat down to calm myself through silent meditation and eventually found some peace as I entered my own depths. I wondered if the restless surface of the ocean knew that it could find peace and tranquility in its own depths. Maybe the ocean heard my thoughts, and as night fell a beautiful moon reflected its light on the waves as if a million diamonds were dancing in joy. The ocean finally seemed at peace.

On this day another common understanding became clearer for me. Our restlessness is caused by events at the superficial level, and the forces are generally external. In the case of the ocean, strong winds created high waves and a very frothy surface. Even then its depths harbored immense peace and tranquility. Similarly, external events that are beyond our control cause anguish, pain, grief, and suffering on the surface while the depths of our soul always remain peaceful. While I always understood this concept intellectually, I now comprehended it spiritually at a much deeper level. The source of our pain is the superficial maya that either eluded us or came to us in abundance. We suffer when we don't possess it because of the paucity of material comforts, especially when we compare ourselves with others who are "blessed" by maya. We suffer when we have an abundance of it because we fear losing it in the future. Similarly, people who are unable to have children of their own can experience depths of sorrow that rival the anguish of those who have children but have suffered the loss of one. In some ways the latter is a worse situation because losing something precious after possessing it can cause excruciating pain, and the emptiness can be overwhelming.

Whether it's a family member whom we lose to addiction, suicide, or estrangement; a child who does not focus on school; a house from which we are evicted due to financial distress; a promotion or a title we do not receive; a lover who leaves us for someone or something else; or a car that's stolen—external objects and people are almost always the sources of grief and sadness.

It is clear that possessing or owning material objects and transient illusions does not bring us peace or happiness, but separation from them, whether temporary or permanent, causes pain and grief. The source of perceived happiness and that of expressed sorrow is the same—maya. I believe most of us, if not all, know this fact intellectually. And yet, we keep pursuing maya with undeterred passion and zeal hoping that perhaps the next thing we buy, love, or attain will eradicate our sorrows. Human evolution is proof that we are naturally wired to adapt ourselves over time to new conditions and new environments. Why is it, then, that we have not been able to learn from repeated failures in our attempt to earn happiness and peace through the traditional means? Why is it that we keep chasing what eludes us when all that's needed is a connection with our own depths? Why is it that we look for answers from prayers, promotions, family members, and friends when all the questions can simply vanish if we find our inner tranquility? And, why is it that even when we do realize the truth of this reality, we are unable to find a way to dismantle our attachments? Perhaps because we are human and we are disconnected from the source of original happiness and peace—our Creator. So, we attach ourselves to things that hold the promise of similar joy. A more spiritual viewpoint is that we need this pain to act as fuel for the fire that will provide the illumination to remove the darkness and take us to the eternal Light. We must pass through all the valleys of pain and suffering before we can begin our ascent to the pristine heights of eternal joy.

Despite the challenges and opposing viewpoints, I find the Kübler-Ross model of five stages of grief easily understandable spiritually. Dr. Kübler-Ross was a Swiss-American psychiatrist who did pioneering work on near-death studies and her five stages of grief model was first discussd in her 1969 book titled *On Death and Dying*. I have experienced some, if not all, of these stages albeit in a different order and sometimes with relapses to earlier stages without moving on to the next one. The model itself has evolved over time since it was initially designed with the input from terminally ill patients. Over the years, it has been adapted to include those grieving the loss of a loved one, the loss of a job, the breakup of two lovers, the news of a chronic or terminal illness, and even the game loss of a favorite sports team. I believe it is important to understand these stages spiritually rather than academically. Science tries to look for evidence to prove the existence of something. Spirituality believes in the existence of something mysterious, something divine, even if it cannot be proven with hard evidence. In fact, that's what some call faith and belief. If we were to be able to explain everything, would anyone need prayer or God or a connection with the Higher Self or spirituality?

The Traditional View: The traditional view on grief and

suffering is adequately expressed through the Kübler-Ross model and has the following five stages of grief:

1. **Denial** is marked by overwhelming sadness and feelings of meaninglessness. It's nature's way of cleansing our soul of the grief and beginning the process of healing. I liken it to applying a stain remover to a deep stain on our favorite piece of clothing. Its job is to break up the stain, even though the whole thing looks hopeless, murky, and unstable. In a way, it's a process to restore the fabric to as close to the original as possible, so the clothing can survive. However, at this stage, we do not believe that the stain will go away. Similarly, denial is a survival mechanism that is designed to make us connect with the raw emotions, even though it makes us hopeless, murky, confused, and not sure if what we are experiencing is actually happening. As the process moves along, the very feelings that our consciousness was denying begin to surface. The first of which is usually anger.

2. **Anger** can be both a strength and a weakness. We've discussed the concept of anger in a chapter dedicated solely to it. Suffice it to say that this destructive force can actually be constructive in destroying what's blocking the healing process. It's like firefighters using

brute force to break through the door to extinguish the fire that rages within. This is one of those situations where anger acts as a catalyst to bring some calm after the storm.

3. **Bargaining** is not a term I am particularly fond of in this context because it reminds me of the power brokers bargaining with the weak simply because they can. It almost seems an exploitive force that demeans and degrades one while elevating the ego of another. I prefer the phrase *finding common ground* that simply states the same without the negative connotations. This is a game the mind plays with us where we are engaged in an "if-then" contest akin to what some do in prayer. "Oh God, if you would grant me this last wish, then I will ... " I remember doing this at the temple in the hospital where my father was recovering. I tried to find common ground with God to heal my father and in return I would not engage in premarital sex. It's a mind game that offers hope for an otherwise improbable solution out of our misery. When results are not forthcoming, depression may start to ensue.

4. **Depression** is another subject we have discussed in some detail in a previous chapter. However, this is a

different kind of depression that occurs naturally after a sense of deep loss, even if it feels unnatural, especially if one had a joyous disposition prior to this loss. This is not the mental illness that some suffer from, but it can escalate into a condition that lasts longer than it should. Some need the support of other loved ones to go through it, some rely on their belief, faith, and prayer, and yet others need professional grief counseling to get through this stage. Either way, this is generally a temporary hole of darkness that eventually gets filled with light, albeit slowly. It's like planting a new seed in the hole left from the uprooting event and then filling it back up. If watered and cared for, the seed will soon sprout, and new growth will soon emerge, which, over time, will help shift our focus to what's new and fresh while the old recedes in our memory.

5. **Acceptance** means coming to terms with the new growth that has emerged from the same place where there was a gaping hole. It is not the same as the old one and it never will be, but it is the new reality, the new normal, if there will ever be such a thing as "normal" with respect to the loss we have suffered. But it is not a compromise, and it never should be. A

compromise essentially means that we have to give up something to accept the new reality. Our life may look and feel different, but it doesn't have to be less than what it was before the loss. It's just different and it will always feel that way. And that's okay. Just because the flower you now have looks and smells different, it doesn't have to be any less beautiful. Clearly, it will take some effort to notice this new beauty because, subconsciously, we will always compare it with what was and lament over what could have been. That's simply human.

The Wah! Perspective: It's important to recognize that simply because you may feel alone, it's not akin to loneliness. Like Osho explains, the former is a state of being that can be filled with love, laughter, and peace while the latter is a state of sadness. Oftentimes, we confuse the two. Loneliness is temporary, but aloneness is permanent— that's how we are born, and that's how we leave this mortal body. Recognizing this difference is important to deal with a sense of loss in a positive way. It's not immediate, but healing does happen. Over time the emotions related to the loss weaken their hold on us, and we learn to accept our new reality.

The new normal can be just as joyous as the past but with new bonds, new viewpoints, new perspectives, and new realities.

Nature, once again, provides inspirational examples to help us lead our life in harmony with whatever situations may befall us. Birds and animals somehow know how to carry on with life despite harsh realities that occur every day.

I recall an especially troubling night emotionally when I was tossing and turning in bed. A thunderstorm had begun around 4:00 a.m., and the lightning clap was so strong that I felt the house shake. My family ran down to the basement, as they are all afraid of lightning and thunder. I lay awake through the storm. Then, amid the howling wind and thunderclaps, a bird began singing to welcome the arrival of the new day. Her song was filled with joy and the promise of light. I wondered if her nest had survived the strong winds and what might have become of her eggs or newborns. The joy in her song was unmistakable despite her new reality. It filled me with a longing desire to be as courageous as that little bird, especially in the face of adversity. I got up at daybreak and wrote down, "Last night, through the thunder, storm, and lightning, I heard a bird sing with unbridled joy and courage. I want to be that bird." These tiny creatures that make the entire sky their home truly know how to live, and they continue to soar despite the pain they may endure. Perhaps there's a reason why. I am reminded of the hymn in the Guru Granth Sahib that my mother used to invoke every time she worried about her children or about the next morning's meal. Her faith in God was unshakable. The hymn, loosely translated, means "Birds fly thousands of miles and leave their babies behind. Who feeds them and who cares for them? They simply chant His name ... "

I am convinced that sooner or later we can recover from our grief and live with similar joy because we are a resilient species and we have evolved over the millennia to adapt to changing circumstances. As evolution forced interrelationships between all forms of life to shift, life marched on and flourished in even the harshest of climates. Life survived and flourished in parched, hot deserts, frozen landmasses, depths of oceans, and even in boiling water that welcomes molten lava into its cool bosom. When, under tremendous pressure, a piece of coal transforms itself into a sparkling diamond, all that changes is the interrelationship of carbon atoms within. The atoms of coal may lament the change in the relationship between and among them, but the new combination produces something even better. What's needed is a new perspective to appreciate this new reality.

But humans have feelings, you may argue, and therefore it's different when something permanently alters our reality. When we experience the loss of a loved one or any other loss for that matter, feelings of sorrow and grief are triggered because our relationship with what we lost is altered permanently. In fact, such an event may even alter the relationship with other aspects of our environment because our very identity may have shifted. These are challenging situations for even the strongest among us. There is one positive, however, that comes from the compassion we show when someone else is in pain. It allows our heart to expand and our soul to feel nourished.

For those who are experiencing the pain and suffering, there are tools they can rely on to make this new reality more comfortable. Prayer, meditation, change of scene, a different job, and new relationships, among others can all be helpful. This does not mean you discard the old. You still preserve it and cherish it the best way you can. At the same time, you find the strength to shift the focus and make a new beginning. After all, changing the external cannot completely change what's inside you. Wherever you go, your thoughts will always be with you. So, while the superficial diversions may help in the short term, stopping and finding a peaceful and restful space inside your being may offer the most durable promise. Prayer, meditation, silence, and reflection can be surprisingly healing. Even prayer has risks if we become dependent on it for our desires. Only the wise pray for the ultimate gift of gratitude and humility.

11

forgiveness, gratitude, humility, and prayer

Earth was parched, and thirsty. Rain showered its love on it. Earth's gratitude rose up as fragrance, one drop at a time.

In 1993 Mary Johnson lost her only child, Laramium Byrd, to a violent homicide. He was twenty years old and did not even know the sixteen-year-old shooter, Oshea Israel, who was convicted of the crime and spent fifteen years in prison. Johnson, inspired by a poem about forgiveness, visited Israel in the prison after a dozen years of bearing the pain of losing her son. Within two hours of meeting him, she was able to truly forgive her son's murderer. She went one step further and adopted him after his release from prison. She went on to found From Death to Life, a support organization for grieving mothers who have lost children to homicide. Johnson, through this organization, encourages forgiveness and reconciliation between the families of murderers and victims.

Johnson was free to make a choice of whether to continue to despise Israel or to forgive him. It's incomprehensible to many how a mother who loses her only son to a senseless crime can not only move on and forgive but open her heart with overwhelming love and compassion for the very person who caused her intense emotional suffering. Social scientists believe that forgiveness is possible in the presence of self-compassion and empathy. When one sees another, even a perpetrator of a heinous crime, with the same sense of compassion as one sees the self, then forgiveness comes easily. Forgiveness, therefore, is a pro-social character strength that is closely linked to loving-kindness or karunā. Social scientists also agree that forgiveness and gratitude are closely related. The gift of forgiveness overwhelmed Israel with gratitude and changed the course of his life for the better. Many such examples exist in history, and simply reading about them or hearing such stories fills us with a sense of peace and a desire to witness more of such goodness all around us.

Cicero, the Greek philosopher, declared several centuries ago: "Gratitude is not only the greatest of virtues, but the parent of all others." The word gratitude has its foundations in the Latin root *gratia* meaning grace, gratefulness, or graciousness. In fact, authors like P.W. Pruyser contend that all derivatives from this root word "have to do with kindness, generousness, gifts, the beauty of giving and receiving, or getting something for nothing." The Latin word *gratus,* meaning pleasing or thankful, is another possible root of the word gratitude. *Gratus* offers the root *grat*—a root that's included in many words like congratulate, ingratiate, and grateful. Words like grace and gravitation also hint at something divine but have the root of *gra* in them. *Gra* is a Gaelic word meaning love. If one were to combine the meaning of the two possible roots of the word gratitude, *gra* and *grat,* you end up with "pleasing love" and "thankful love." This meaning, in my opinion, is much closer to the definition of gratitude.

The world's major religions and belief systems, like Hinduism, Islam, Judaism, Buddhism, Sikhism, and Christianity consider gratitude a prized human emotion. Even a scientific phenomenon like earth's gravity has love as its foundation. Perhaps that's why we use the name Mother Earth that emanates love for everything through gravity. She accepts any and all and absorbs them in her bosom with love, gratitude, and humility. With her love even excrement turns into manure that enriches plant life and produces flowers and fruits. Plants, in turn, not only spread unspeakable beauty, but they also support other life forms. Only a mother can have such a big heart filled with overwhelming love that it can transform even the discarded to the accepted, hated to the loved, ugly to the beautiful, insipid to the most delicious. That's why I consider the mother as the Creator.

My father used to say that a fruit that hangs closest to the ground is juiciest and most ripe. It took me a long time to appreciate his viewpoint about humility. Many create an inextricable link between gratitude and humility as symbiotic virtues that promote and enhance each other. Bowing down, in many cultures, is a humble gesture to express respect to elders, to gurus, and to God. It's no wonder, therefore, that the root word for humility is the Latin word *humilis,* meaning low. Towering mountains get their status because of the low valleys attached to them. It is in the low depths of earth that diamonds are formed. The most beautiful structures we admire would not be able to stand if it weren't for the stones that formed the foundations below the surface. This is the "low" that my father explained so eloquently through the metaphor of the low-hanging fruit.

More recently, as the stresses of modern life have taken a toll on the human condition, researchers have investigated the concept of gratitude in both scientific and unscientific ways to measure its effects on our physiological and emotional well-being. An overwhelming majority of such studies, such as those conducted by pre-eminent gratitude researchers like Dr. Robert Emmons and by Chopra Foundation, have reached the same conclusion—gratitude, as a feeling, emotion, attitude, or a moral virtue, has far-reaching positive effects on some of the most desirable states of being. Researchers, ministers, priests, lay people, and even some world leaders agree that lasting happiness, good health, forgiveness, compassion, inner peace, and overall well-being results from the conscious practice of expressing gratitude. In fact, gratitude may also have the power to neutralize some negative emotions like anger, anxiety, and depression, some studies show. What's consistent in all these studies is that there needs to be an external catalyst to arouse the feeling of gratitude because such an emotion is expressed *toward something,* even if that "something" is one's breath, God, a flower, a relationship, and even material wealth. Perhaps most encouraging is the fact that scientific observations show that gratitude can be cultivated and enhanced through several daily practices like writing a gratitude journal or being thankful in one's daily prayer.

Humility is defined in the Merriam-Webster Dictionary as "the quality or state of not thinking you are better than other people; freedom from pride or arrogance; the quality of state of being humble." The Oxford Dictionary states humility as "a modest or low view of one's own importance." What's clear from these definitions is that humility is both a state of being that can be experienced by the self and can also be observed by another. In other words, humility is akin to a vibration that travels through space and is felt by another through mere observation. It is also a state of being felt by people who genuinely feel that they are nothing special and that there are many others better than they. Of all the definitions and explanations, I find the one by Dr. Karl Albrecht, a coach, author, and an executive management consultant to be the most insightful. In his article "The Paradoxical Power of Humility," published in *Psychology Today* he writes:

"Humility is about emotional neutrality. It involves an experience of growth in which you no longer need to put yourself above others, but you don't put yourself below them, either. Everyone is your peer—from the most 'important' person to the least. You're just as valuable as every other human being on the planet, no more and no less. It's about behaving and reacting from purposes, not emotions. You learn to simply disconnect or de-program the competitive reflex in situations where it's not productive... Humility is less a matter of self-restraint and more a matter of self-esteem. The greater your sense of self-worth, the easier it is to appreciate others, to praise them, and to encourage them."

In yet another scientific study, authored by Kruse, Chancellor, Ruberton, and Lyubomirsky, the findings show a mutually reinforcing and upward spiraling link between gratitude and humility.

Clearly, there's widespread agreement about the benefits of cultivating and promoting the virtues of gratitude and humility. While all these studies show a direct link, I attempt to answer the question *why*? Why do gratitude and humility lead to so many positive results in the human condition? What is the reason that Cicero called gratitude the parent of all emotions? Did he know something more at a deeper level, or was the use of the word *parent* purely coincidental?

In my research, I could not find any scientific studies that have dealt with this question. Even if there were some studies that attempted to better understand the reasons behind the beneficial effects of humility and gratitude, the answers would have likely come only in the form of theory or hypothesis. The theory that would likely be most convincing would be the one that delved deep into the human psyche from a spiritual angle since it is hard to pinpoint the source of our emotions, even if we can localize them in a particular region of our brain.

I believe there are important clues hidden in the effects created by gratitude and humility that hold the keys to this mystery. Let's consider one common thread among all the positive effects of gratitude and humility: they are universally associated with feelings of happiness and inner peace. Why is that the case?

The answer is almost too simple. Effects that gratitude and humility can create—qualities like forgiveness, compassion, altruism, loving-kindness, equanimity, peacefulness, patience, and self-control—are all synonymous with "Godlike" attributes. The universality of the high value placed by almost all religions on gratitude and humility, therefore, is no coincidence. These qualities help us connect with our Creator through a mechanism that's self-reinforcing. The more we practice gratitude and humility, the more peaceful we feel. The reason why we feel more peaceful, in my opinion, is because the vibrations in our subconscious are likely similar to how we must have felt when we were in our mother's womb—grateful, peaceful, patient, and full of love. We were one with our Creator in that state. We were not in any competition against anyone. We had nothing to prove. We were simply present—breathing and growing through our Creator, our mother.

Gratitude and humility evoke the same feelings and state of being as a child in her mother's womb. Once again, we feel connected with our Creator. The positive side effects of these virtues, therefore, act as the detergent to wash off the dirt that we had accumulated over the years. The more we practice gratitude and humility, the more cleansing we experience. The more cleansing there is, the more Light reveals itself from deep under the layers of darkness. We become capable of shedding our emotional baggage because we feel the support and love of our Creator. It's no wonder that people who practice gratitude and humility regularly become better leaders, lose addictions through self-control, and are warmly accepted, and even sought, by all those around them. *The Gap* narrows, the darkness starts to abate, and we become closer to the source of Light.

Even a simple examination of the lives of the enlightened

souls—both historical and contemporaneous—reveals that their lives were seeped in gratitude and humility. If we ache to find the kind of peace these enlightened teachers found in their journey through the mortal life, then we must also embrace the values they espoused and lived by—and died for.

The more gratitude and humility we feel, the closer we become with God, our Creator. That's what our consciousness seeks as it searches for durable peace and lasting happiness. It is noteworthy, but not surprising, that neither gratitude nor humility has anything to do with maya or the material illusion. In fact, one could argue that these two virtues slowly eat away at and destroy the illusion of maya by working in invisible depths of our being and cleansing our soul. They nourish our soul just like the deep roots silently feed the entire tree and bring about unbound growth, fruits, flowers, and fragrance. The fruit tree does not care what it looks like, it simply grows and gives itself completely and selflessly to the world. There's no competition, hatred, jealousy, envy, anger, or anxiety—just peaceful existence filled with pure, selfless love. That's exactly what we feel when we are in the company of a person seeped in the virtuous glory of gratitude and humility. People who are spiritually awakened describe similar feelings when they are one with the Creator. This knowledge alone can show us the path to wisdom.

How can we become more forgiving, grateful, and humble? Prayer and meditation may hold the key because, as studies show, they are closely linked to gratitude.

Prayer is that mysterious channel in which our soul and the spirit of the Creator vibrate together in a harmonious song that brings peace, joy, and calm to mortal beings. Prayer, whether motivated by hope, fear, superstition, duty, or belief system, has one common attribute—it's a mode of communication between a mortal and the Sublime. It does not have to be performed in a place of worship or be part of a religious order. The religious, the spiritual, and the atheists alike can engage in prayer that fits their way of life and ideology.

However, prayer can affect our consciousness in both positive and negative ways. When prayer is offered from a place of fear, it can have a negative affect on our psyche. Some religions espouse the concept of heaven and hell, of the final day of reckoning when good and bad deeds will be accounted for, of prize and punishment based on our deeds. Prayer, in such religions, is motivated by either fear or hope—fear of being banished to hell or hope of being elevated to heaven. Either approach can sometimes lead to radicalism with disastrous effects. While most people associate prayer with something peaceful and good, radicalism can shift that focus to violence and terror.

Prayer can also take the form of a conscious intention to effect change and embrace self-love. It was during the family constellation work conducted by Ron Young, a renowned spiritual healer, as part of the curriculum at Columbia University, that I was able to purge a large part of the guilt, shame, and grief associated with my father's suicide. The catharsis I experienced that day in the Catskills, over 28 years after my father's passing, shook my soul's foundation to its core, and the resulting cracks began releasing the long-subdued pain in a manner that no therapy or medicine could ever do. I believe that day placed me on a more durable journey of healing as opposed to staying stuck in quicksand.

The most amazing part of this healing journey is that no traditional form of prayer was involved in it. Only a desire and an intention to bare my soul to the moment in which I saw my father standing in front of me when I asked him to forgive me for all my shortcomings and to love me. His tearful, loving embrace triggered a tsunami of grief that I had never experienced before. I knew he had forgiven me, and I was finally able to tell him the four simple words that I never had the courage to utter while he was alive: *I love you, Dad.*

Prayer became intention that day—intention for forgiving the self. The responsibility of forgiving myself was no longer passed on to my Creator. It became my own. I was finally able to see that God has only a loving side, because my dad embodied God that day! None of my acts were sinful to him. They were sinful only to my conscience, to my superego, as Freud would conclude. Now I pray with a different frame of mind, one that is always peaceful and always intentional. It's part of my daily meditation.

Regardless of how each of us feels about prayer, scientific studies are proving the immense power that religion and spirituality, the harbingers of prayer and meditation, can have to literally rewire our brain. Scientists have shown that the cortical thickness of the brain increases over time in those who make meditation a daily and significant part of their life. The thickening of the cerebral cortex is known to protect against the ill effects of depression and anxiety. In fact, meditation and prayer impact the entire neurotransmitter system in such a manner that it significantly reduces the symptoms associated with anxiety and depressive disorders. Such is the power of meditative prayer associated with religion and spirituality. However, it must be noted that not all those who are spiritual are also religious and vice versa; additionally, not all those who are spiritual engage in the practice of prayer while most who are religious make prayer an important part of their life. Prayer and meditation are also not exactly alike. If prayer induces a meditative state of mind, then the benefits it generates on the brain are clear. However, not all practices of praying have been shown to have the same effect on the human brain as meditation does. Clearly, a lot more work needs to be done in this area to better understand the psychology of prayer, especially when it becomes a meditative practice.

Prayer is a private dialogue between our absolute true self and either an inner guide or an external Higher Life, God, Creator, or Deity. Prayer is that safe mode of personal communication during which we can bare our darkest secrets and the most intimate part of our conscience without the fear of being judged by others of our own kind. Prayer has its own code that only our own soul can decipher. It is cryptic and it is simple at the same time. We often don't share this code with even the closest of our family and friends—our spouse, parents, siblings, or childhood friends. For many, prayer is their closest friend, even in death, like it was for my mother. Prayer is the Light that leads them out of darkness. It is their teacher, guide, inspiration, guru. In order to shift the frame of life effectively, we need the help of a guru, guide, teacher, or source of inspiration. Such a guru can be found in a person, the scriptures, in nature, in our passions, and even in silence.

12

Gu-Ru—out of darkness, into the Light

When His Light passes through the prism of our soul, our life is enriched with a rainbow of blessings. Only an authentic soul can witness the rainbow in all its glory!

Darkness and Light have been used as metaphors in various religions to explain spirituality and the concept of our Creator, Higher Self, Inner Self, God, or Supreme Power. Even atheists have expressed their beliefs in the context of these two words. Philosophers alike have deployed them in their writings to contextualize their viewpoints.

One of the earliest words in religious and spiritual writings that signifies the concept of Darkness and Light is the Sanskrit word *guru.* While the more generalized meaning of this word is "teacher," it is considered far weightier in its contextual meaning. When thought of as a teacher, it signifies a wise person who is deeply connected to his or her soul, who guides his or her disciples in the understanding of life's bigger questions, values, and experiential systems; someone who explains the meaning of life and how to achieve lasting peace and happiness.

Guru has its roots in the Sanskrit word *gri,* which means to invoke, or to praise. It is also likely connected to the word *gur,* which signifies to raise, to lift up. In Hinduism, the reference to guru comes from verse 16 in the Upanishads, where the syllable *gu* means darkness and the syllable *ru* means he who dispels the darkness. Guru, or the spiritual teacher is, therefore, someone who can take us out of darkness and into the Light. In the context of this definition of guru, Darkness means ignorance, physical or emotional suffering, and cravings for maya, while Light signifies the removal of the fragmentation in our soul and its unification into one whole so we can find lasting peace.

In Buddhism, especially Tibetan Buddhism, guru is known as the *Vajra Guru,* which literally means the *diamond guru.* Tantras consider Guru as an embodiment of Buddha himself and, therefore, Guru is a figure worthy of worship and following. Darkness, in Buddhism, is the innate craving for the transient and the impermanent that prevents mortals from achieving enlightenment, even when one has the potential to see the Light, the real Truth, and achieve salvation from the dark cycle of birth and death.

Of all the religions, Sikhism has perhaps used the word guru most prominently by adding it as a prefix to the names of each of its prophets, including its final guide or guru, the scriptures called Guru Granth Sahib. The word guru and its root *gur* finds prolific use in Guru Granth Sahib with the same significance as found in the Upanishads—*gu* meaning darkness and *ru* meaning Light that dispels the darkness. Sikhs call this Light, the *jot* or Divine Light. All Sikh gurus, therefore, were the embodiment of the Divine Light as the *jot* was passed on from one to the next until its final resting place in the Sikh Holy Scriptures, Guru Granth Sahib. *Granthis,* or priests in the gurudwara are charged with spreading this Light to others through the singing of hymns, discourses, and chants of *Waheguru. Wah-e-Guru* is an expression that signifies wonderment at guru's creation and guidance. Through its chanting, Sikhs meditate on this Creation and express their appreciation and wonder at the small miracles that surround them everywhere.

In Judaism, Light is the genesis that created the world as is clear from the answer that the Midrash, the rabbinic literature, offers in response to the question, "From what was light created?" The answer is in Genesis Rabbah 3:4: "G-d cloaked Himself in a white shawl, and the light of its splendor shone from one end of the world to the other." Judaism, like many other religions, considers Light to be fundamentally beautiful and positive. Hence, the significance of light in many religions where candles, lamps, and other forms of light signify purity, divinity, and all that is good. Biblical Hebrew utilizes the metaphor of the word "shine" to denote everything from redemption, truth, justice, peace, and even life itself.

Christianity is replete with similar examples where the metaphor of Light and Darkness has been used to explain the same concepts of good and evil, virtue and folly, pure God and sinful humanity. The New Testament says, "The Light shines in the darkness, and the darkness has not overcome it," in John 1:5; and "But if anyone walks in the night, he stumbles, because the Light is not in him," in John 11:10.

In Islam, the word used for Light is *nūr,* which comes from the same root as the Hebrew *aor,* or the Primal Light described in the Book of Genesis. The Holy Quran uses the word *nūr* or its derivatives forty-nine times to describe God, Prophet Muhammad, the Quran itself, the moon, and men and women of faith. The phrase *nurun 'ala nūr,* or *Light Upon Light* is often used by Muslims to describe the infinite and glorious Light of Allah or God. In fact, the derivative *Al-nūr* is used together with *zulumat,* or darkness, to illustrate the movement from darkness into light, from ignorance into faith. Finally, to Sufis, Light signifies our awareness about our Inner Self while darkness means what we do not know.

While the metaphor of darkness and Light is prevalent in every popular religion, it is important to address how we may find our own unique way, our path to move from suffering and pain (darkness) to a state of lasting peace and joy (Light). Many of us are so scared and often paralyzed by the darkness in our lives that we completely surrender to its power. Addiction, anxiety, depression, anger, hostility, envy, hate, jealousy, competition, greed, lust, and hubris are all examples of darkness in our lives because each of these emotions disturbs our peace and, therefore, removes us from what we seek as our ultimate goal— lasting happiness. While happiness is rarely a permanent state of being, we are deprived of even a glimpse of it when darkness envelops our life. We seek Light, but we find ourselves trapped in the web of darkness time and time again.

However, there's hope. The fact that we can see darkness is evidence of light behind it. Darkness cannot reveal itself in the dark. It's virtually impossible. Darkness, therefore, is simply an absence of light. All we need to do is to turn on our inner Light. The question is how? How do we move past our addictions, the lure of the material, the sensual pleasures, the comforts that surround us, the beauty that attracts us, and a society that propels us to achieve more of all that is material, transient, and illusory? Many of us recognize these enticements but still get caught in doubt, theories, thoughts, webs of reason, and our own duality. How do we break these shackles and liberate ourselves from maya not just for the sake of freedom from it but for the ultimate goal of finding peace and tranquility? How do we sacrifice ourselves like the waterfall without losing our song and our yearning to merge joyously with something bigger than ourselves? How do we become a bird that can sing with unbridled joy and courage even during a ferocious storm?

Mikhail Naimy in *The Book of Mirdad* offers a simple solution to find our inner Light, but he also gives a warning with regard to our darkness (ego) getting in the way. He says, "As is your Consciousness, therefore, so is your I. As is your I, so is your world. If it be clear and definite of meaning, your world is clear and definite of meaning; and then your words should never be a maze; nor should your deeds be ever nests of pain. If it be hazy and uncertain, your world is hazy and uncertain; and then your words are but entanglements; and then your deeds are hatcheries of pain." How does one achieve this harmony between our Inner Self, our words, and our deeds so that they are reflections of our true and authentic consciousness?

At the practical level, my answer may not be your answer. In fact, there are many paths to the same place we are all seeking. I have tried many and found, like many others, that the choice of solutions is bewildering. Since most of us are seeking dramatic results in a short period of time, we keep shifting from one technique to another before giving any of them a durable chance. Rather than focus on digging a deep hole in which we can bury our darkness, we keep digging several shallow ones that are inept at accommodating the enormity of our misery.

Another challenge we encounter is that some of these solutions require either complex methodologies or an inordinate amount of time and practice, or impractical solutions that are not compatible with family and work life. While I cannot overemphasize the importance of silence and meditation, it is difficult for most of us to "just be" or "go within" or "find our Inner Self" with any regularity, and the results, oftentimes, are temporary because *maya* keeps pulling us in different directions.

Clearly, achieving the state of mental peace that is devoid of judgment; finding joy in every moment, in every action and every thing around us; becoming comfortable with ourselves and being alone as opposed to being lonely; developing humility; and graciously practicing gratitude and compassion at every opportunity is the end goal. I believe that the path we follow should be pragmatic and lead us to the peaceful place that enlightened souls like Buddha, Jesus, Guru Nanak, Mahavira, Mohammed, and others were trying to show us through their personal experiences. This path does not have to take us to the solitude of the Himalayas or to ashrams or monasteries, even though that is a way some will take. In fact, almost all the gurus warn against it. The process, therefore, should be simple enough that anyone with a desire to find peace and tranquility can do it almost instinctively and with devoted passion.

Each of us must, however, write our own story and carve our unique path on this journey to remove the darkness and to find the Inner Light. As dim as the Light may be, it's still better than darkness. There's only one condition: that our soul be authentic. Only then will His Light enrich our life with a rainbow of blessings that will bring peace, awe, happiness, and contentment. Even a slight bit of inauthenticity will cause the rainbow to lose some of its colors. Imagine what a rainbow in the sky would look like if the color blue or red were blocked from its spectrum. It would appear inauthentic. Similarly, our life's richness can become devoid of all its glory if anger, ego, lust, or envy were to block His Light.

So, here is the surprisingly simple understanding of my personal calling. While I am convinced that it has shown me the path to potentially end suffering or at least suppress its seeds and move toward lasting peace and tranquility, you will need to reach your own conclusion. To be sure, it won't be an island of peace one resides on permanently, but the instances of eternal joy will become more frequent and longer lasting in our lives if we put into practice this universal solution that enlightened gurus hinted at in their guidance to the mortal souls.

The insight that I received through the Light's blessing is that my journey does not begin inside me or through me. It begins with the compassionate recognition that not only does everyone suffer but each person's suffering is just as real and painful as my own. **I believe karunā, or the genuine desire to remove someone else's pain, holds the key to the door that will liberate us from maya's dark prison. I am convinced that selfless compassion for those who are helpless and suffering deeply is the way to dispel the darkness from my Gap and find my Inner Light. I believe that by helping heal the pain and suffering of others and by witnessing the resulting relief, I will find the secret potion that will eventually wipe out my own darkness.** And I want to be utterly greedy and selfish with karunā. I want my inner being to be filled with so much selfless compassion, that it has no place else to go but to overflow to others.

It is for this reason that I now serve abandoned children who have suffered unspeakable sexual and physical abuse. My hope is to provide them with enough skill sets and grit that they can have a fair shot at a sustainable life. I went through a similar experience during my childhood, but I had the support of many along the way to become financially and emotionally independent. That was an important step to launch my journey toward personal healing and a holistic existence. Now it's my turn to offer the same hope to these children who have no one else to turn to. They must find the store of inner strength to continue their life's journey with passion and joy. All they need is genuine concern, relentless compassion, and warm love. As they progress through life and achieve emotional and financial stability, my journey toward holistic peace will automatically move forward with them. A break in their vicious cycle of pain, suffering, abuse, and poverty will kindle a virtuous cycle of joy, peace, and contentment in all our lives. I am sure of it as I am already witnessing the divine rainbow in the smiles of some. My observations are supported by the extensive body of research on compassion, specifically self-compassion, that Dr. Kristin Neff, Professor of Human Development and Culture at the University of Texas at Austin, has created over the last decade.

My personal search for Guru has finally ended. These children are my Gu-Ru because they are leading me out of darkness and into the Light. Their innocence and raw genuineness has the essence of God, and it has the strange but calming effect of connecting me with my own Creator. They are the purest of mirrors through which I can reflect upon my own life and find the dark spots that still need cleaning up. My gratitude to these innocent souls is beyond the expression of words. They have given me hope when everything seemed dismal and dark all around me. They have given meaning to my life when it felt sapped of any purpose. They have given me inner happiness, joy, and smiles that had left me without notice. They have shown me the Light.

I believe it is for this reason that every enlightened soul showed us the path of compassion and empathy. Guru Nanak called it *sewa,* or service to others. Buddha called it karunā, or the desire to remove pain from others' lives. The Theravada branch of Buddhism includes three other states of being besides karunā: *metta,* or the desire to bring happiness and joy to others; *mudita,* or sympathetic joy when one truly rejoices in the happiness of others; and *upeksha* or equanimity. Once all four states are present, one can attain enlightenment, which is nothing more than a tool to process pain and suffering with compassion, self-love, and equanimity.

Perhaps the word for compassion in Hebrew is the closest that accords some validity to my theory of absolute peace in the mother's womb. That word is *rachamim,* which comes from the root word *rechem,* meaning the womb! Finally, Sri Patanjali captured the essence of this secret in one of his Yoga Sutras, or threads, as early as 5,000 B.C. to 300 A.D. He wrote in Sanskrit, *"Maitri Karunā muditopeksānām sukha duhkha punyāpunya visayānam bhāvanātas citta prasādanam."* Translated by Sri

Swami Satchidananda in *The Yoga Sutras of Patanjali,* this sutra means "By cultivating attitudes of friendliness toward the happy, compassion for the unhappy, delight in the virtuous, and disregard toward the wicked, the mind-stuff retains its undisturbed calmness." It is perhaps the most profound passage that Sri Patanjali wrote because it gave us the secret of finding our own happiness. It is strangely similar to the four states of being that Buddha prescribed for an enlightened soul.

Nature has always given me answers and inspiration. Its selfless compassion was on display during a recent trip to the Arenal Volcano in Costa Rica. During a leisurely hike that lasted over two hours, the guide explained why the trees grow so tall in the rainforests. He logically offered the scientific reason that trees continue to rise until they break through the forest's canopy to get as much sunlight as possible so they can survive. It's survival of the fittest, he reasoned. On the trunks and branches of these trees are hundreds of varieties of plants flourishing in a peaceful, almost divine way. How do these plants survive without the sunlight? I asked myself. Scientists may say that these plants have adapted themselves to darkness and don't need light. I wonder whether trees follow nature's tall order so that they can survive, or do they rise over the forest's canopy so they can provide their own sap to those who cannot? Is it truly survival of the fittest, or is it yet another example of nature's immense compassion? If the tree does not survive, the others who are so intimately connected to its trunk and branches would perish for sure. I believe the tree's soul knows this stark truth and does everything in its power to give the gift of life to many others who are not equipped to survive on their own—the ferns, orchids, lichens and cacti, among many others. Much of the plant life that is necessary for the biodiversity and richness of the dark rainforest depends on a few tall trees to reach the skies for the light. Scientists give these phenomena fancy name like mutualism or mutualistic symbiosis. I believe it's pure love and karunā in plain sight! In fact, I believe that the tree does not see the "parasites" on its trunks and branches as different from its own soul—it sees its own spirit in them. It sees everything as one.

The examples of such symbiotic karunā in nature are all around us—birds eating insects off animals' backs, ostriches and zebras collaborating to avoid predators, and the "crocodile bird" entering the jaws of death to provide dental hygiene to the crocodile. What drives them to this relationship? How could it be anything other than selfless compassion? I wonder what the world could be like if those among us who have become tall and mighty could offer this karunā to those who don't have a way of getting any light because of the big shadows of the powerful. There are many who are devoting their lives to doing just that, but we need a groundswell if we are to have any hope of moving the needle on suffering among the poor, abused, abandoned, and orphaned. So that humanity can also achieve the biodiversity and the richness it is capable of, just like the rainforests.

To achieve a similar harmony in our lives, all we have to do is to reflect deeply on the words of the enlightened souls in our own unique way through meditation, music, art, dance, sitting in silence, or by selflessly serving others. I am convinced beyond any doubt that the joy of giving selflessly will act as the cleanser to purify our spirit and reveal our true authentic soul. Serving those who need our help most will be my personal cleanser. However, I must be willing to break my toughest chains—my own vulnerabilities, my fears, my ego, and my duality. I must have the courage to face my own truth so that I can dispose of the garbage I have collected over the years and allow my authenticity to emerge naturally. And that is perhaps the most difficult task because it will reveal the ugliness that frightens many of us. When processed constructively, the results could be miraculously sweet—just like a tree takes all the dead material in the ground and turns it into fragrant flowers and delicious fruits. I want to witness the abandoned and the abused children transform their lives' dead material into something fragrant and beautiful. Witnessing this transformation will allow my life's tree to bear its own flowers and fruits once again. Then, and only then, can I begin this journey in earnest—like the river dancing and rejoicing, even in darkness and through dangerous terrain, on its journey to merge with her true Creator, the ocean. So, I can find my final resting place in my own tranquil depths.

You might ask, what's at stake for me or for anyone desirous of following this path? With a traditional worldview that uses the lens colored by maya—everything! But using the compassionate *Wah!* perspective with an understanding of our own mortality—nothing! The more important question is what's at stake for the helpless children and, in a larger sense for humanity as a whole, if we all stay in the fake and transient cocoon of material wealth and sensual pleasures? This is the bigger question we each have to ask ourselves in our own distinctive way and let the answer come to us, and it will if we have purity and authenticity in our spirit.

The other question one may ask is what does one stand to gain from this quest? I come from the world of finance and investments where one number—rate of return, or ROR—measures success. The roar of ROR is so loud that one can easily lose one's own voice, absent the conscious awareness of our life's purpose. So, what's the ROR for someone like me in this work of selfless compassion to help those who need our help most? I don't believe any number can answer this question. The ROR in this work cannot be measured because I stand to win back my authenticity, my soul, my own truth. As a result I will likely be a better person, dad, spiritual partner, and friend. Many spend their entire lifetime gaping into the darkness for this Light, but only a few receive the blessings of the Supreme Being. I have spent much of my life in such an abyss and have engaged in actions that I am not particularly proud of because they have caused tremendous pain to my family and to my own soul. A return to my true spirit so I can love myself again is better than any measurable rate of return. And for the abandoned and forgotten children as well, the ROR has the potential to be life-changing. I recognize that we won't be able to change the world or give every child a bright future. That's an unrealistic goal.

As my father taught me, we may not be able to change the world but we can certainly try to change the world of a few who are less fortunate. Sometimes changing even one life is good enough for a lifetime. That's how I want to remember my father. This one's for you, Dad. I love you, and I miss you!

ABOUT THE AUTHOR

On the surface I am a successful entrepreneur in the financial services industry. I am a well-recognized public speaker in the not-for-profit world of finance. I have two amazing daughters, a group of enviable friends and what everyone would consider to be a fairly normal and comfortable lifestyle. I arrived in the United States with dreams and fears as big as the Titanic and The Universe successfully steered my life's ship through all kinds of storms. I was able to achieve the coveted American Dream and more, for which I am eternally grateful.

Despite the worldly success, I felt empty inside as if something was missing. I simply could not put my finger on it. Like many others, I had an aching gap in my soul that was filled with all kinds of existential questions but no answers. What's the purpose of my life? Why do I not feel fulfilled and happy despite all the material success? How can I find a more durable way of overcoming suffering and finding peace and joy? On the urging of my family, I saw therapists for grief counseling related to my father's suicide and to come to terms with complex feelings of shame and guilt connected with my personal sexual abuse as an adolescent. I got temporary comfort from prayer, meditation, and counseling but the gap did not heal.

Starting in 2009, I started to experience channel openings that delivered answers to some of my questions albeit in small bites. They were enough to give me hope. The watershed moment occurred in January 2016 during a deep meditation which completely changed the way I viewed human suffering in this material world. This book is an endeavor to share my personal insights and awakenings. I hope that my small kernels of truth will trigger a spark inside you or inform your journey to discover your own truth.

All profits from the sale of this book will be donated to support the work I do with abandoned and sexually abused children. Your support will help make the difference. I call it, *Heal to Help Heal.*

Proof

Made in the USA
Columbia, SC
24 February 2018